MAYA
IN
EXILE

Temple University Press

PHILADELPHIA

MAYA IN EXILE

GUATEMALANS IN FLORIDA

Allan F. Burns

INTRODUCTION BY

Jerónimo Camposeco

Temple University Press, Philadelphia 19122
Copyright © 1993 by Temple University. All rights reserved
Published 1993
Printed in the United States of America

The paper used in this publication meets the minimum
requirements of American National Standard for
Information Sciences—Permanence of Paper for Printed
Library Materials, ANSI Z39.48-1984 ⊗

Library of Congress Cataloging-in-Publication Data
Burns, Allan F. (Allan Frank), 1945–
    Maya in exile: Guatemalans in Florida / Allan F. Burns:
    introduction by Jerónimo Camposeco.
        p.   cm.
    Introd. in English and Spanish.
    Includes bibliographical references (p.   ) and index.
    ISBN 1-56639-035-4 (cloth: alk. paper). —
    ISBN 1-56639-036-2 (paper: alk. paper)
    1. Kanjobal Indians—Social conditions.   2. Mayas—
Social conditions.   3. Indiantown (Fla.)—Social
conditions.   4. Refugees, Political—Guatemala.
5. Refugees, Political—Florida.   I. Title.
F1465.2.K36B87   1993
305.897′4—dc20   92-22774

Jessica and Christopher Burns
Julie Gray Burns
Peter and Marcia Burns
Barbara and Peter McGrath
Aldona and Peter Burns
Alex and Virginia Burneik
Petras Burneikas and Alexandra Savikas
Frank and Beatrice Dalidonas

CONTENTS

PREFACE

The Maya have endured to become the most numerous indigenous group on the North American continent. Over four million Maya live in the lowlands of the Yucatan Peninsula, in the
highlands of Chiapas, in Guatemala, and now, in the United
States. Beginning in the early 1980s hundreds of thousands of
Maya fled the terror of Guatemalan civil strife to safety in
Mexico and the United States. Mexico, already burdened with
an economic crisis, has recognized only forty-six thousand of
these people as refugees; other Guatemalan refugees, estimated
at between two and six hundred thousand, live a shadow existence in the cities and rural hamlets.

The lack of refugee assistance in Mexico has driven some
Maya to the United States. By the 1990s Mexico had instituted
the policy of actively interdicting and deporting Guatemalans
who were not registered as part of the initial group of forty-six
thousand. Using the networks founded by a few pioneers who
left Guatemala in the 1970s and established communities in
Houston and Los Angeles, Maya fleeing the turmoil of their
homeland in the 1980s began to settle in the United States
rather than Mexico. Soon small towns in Florida became a
Guatemalan Maya migration goal. By the 1990s Florida was
recognized as a key center of the new Maya communities in the
United States.

As word of a Florida community called "El Pueblo de los

Indios," or "Indiantown," reached Guatemala, more refugees came. By 1987 the seemingly unstoppable migration into Indiantown had created a crisis for the small community. Overcrowding, alcoholism, and increasing notoriety caused longtime residents to begin to view the immigrant Maya as a liability. They were no longer seen as refugees but as poor farmworkers who depleted local resources. By the 1990s Indiantown had become an ambivalent cultural center for the Maya. It was considered the community that offered the best opportunity for cultural survival in the United States, yet it suffered from a severe shortage of housing and social services and a native population that was increasingly hostile toward what many now termed the "invasion" from Central America. As the decade of the nineties began, the possibility of returning to a normal life in Guatemala continued to elude the Maya. The Maya in Florida today are made up of many who have applied for political asylum, many who have legal documents allowing them to work under the farmworker provisions of the Immigration Reform and Control Act of 1986, and many who are illegal aliens.

This volume is an account of how the Maya from Guatemala have adjusted to immigrant life in the United States. The emphasis is on the Maya as a new U.S. ethnic group, one that is torn between a profound history of civilization in Central America, the horror of bloody campaigns carried out against these people by their own government, and the uncertain status of the Maya here in the United States. On the one hand, the indigenous nature of this refugee community makes it unique in the current context of United States immigration, but on the other hand, the Guatemalan Maya share with earlier refugees the exuberance and misfortune of being outsiders in an unfamiliar land. My own grandparents told similar stories about their escape from Lithuania at the turn of the century, and today Lithuania's move toward liberty is appreciated by many of the Maya in the United States.

This book has its roots in applied anthropology work with the Maya of Florida. I was first contacted by some of the Florida Maya in 1983 to help with their adaptation to Florida, and I subsequently carried out scholarship and advocacy with the community. The book is written as a testimony to the efforts the Maya have made to contribute to the United States as new immigrants and to retain the strength of their culture.

I have used pseudonyms throughout the book except for the name of my colleague and collaborator, Jerónimo Camposeco, a Jacaltec Maya, and the names of the students at the University of Florida who worked in the community over the years. Many of the Kanjobal Maya use what appear to be first names as family names, so "Eulalia Francisco" is a possible Kanjobal first and last name. I have followed this practice in creating pseudonyms for this book.

In 1987 the Guatemalan legislature passed a law, which was subsequently signed by then-president Vinicio Cerezo, regularizing the orthography of Maya languages in Guatemala. I have retained the older spelling of "Kanjobal" rather than the newer "Q'anjob'al" in this volume, as it is still the term most recognized in the United States and, as Jerónimo Camposeco points out in the Introduction, the term most often used by the Kanjobal Maya themselves. The difference points to an evolving separation between the Maya of the United States and the Maya of Guatemala.

As I write this, the festival of the patron saint of the Kanjobal Maya is being held at the county park in Indiantown. There is talk of an epidemic of encephalitis being carried by mosquitos this year, and the autumn rains have turned the park into mud. The weather is hot and humid and mosquitos are everywhere. Still, thousands of Guatemalans, both Maya and "ladinos" or non-Maya, come to the park to see what is happening at the fiesta. Francisco Manuel, a refugee I have known for several years, has sought me out to give me a cassette tape he recorded when he went back to Guatemala last year. It is a tape of voices and music from the fiesta held in Guatemala where Pedro Francisco performed as an expert marimba player. He gave me the tape to demonstrate that although he has to return to Guatemala surreptitiously to play the marimba, it sounds much better when he plays it in Guatemala than it does when he plays it in Florida.

ACKNOWLEDGMENTS

The cultural research for this book was possible only because I have had the good fortune to teach at the University of Florida. There I met many students, both undergraduate and graduate, who sharpened my ideas, went to Indiantown to do their own research and advocacy, and discussed the issues of refugees and immigrants through many hours of conversations, seminars, and classes. I am fortunate to be able to teach in a university where students bring curiosity and enthusiasm to the classroom. Maria Cecilia Rocha, Maria Miralles, Joan Flocks, Manuel Vargas, Alfredo Gonzalez, Sherri Dorman, Greg Mac-Donald, Randi Cameon, Andrea Stebor, and Julian Arturo were among the students who carried out important, long-term research in the community. Denise Matthews, Olivia Carrescia, and Alan Saperstein are three filmmakers whose ideas and compassion for people were important to the documentaries that were made about the Maya. They also taught me visual literacy. The combination of theoretical wisdom, political vision, and culture brokering skills characterize Jerónimo Camposeco and Anna Camposeco, to whom I owe a debt of friendship and gratitude. Even through the crises of life between Guatemala and Florida, the Camposecos have shown great strength. Pedro Francisco, Maria Mendez, Antonio Silvestre, Andres Cruz, Dominga Cruz, and many other friends and colleagues in Indiantown have given me the chance to understand the Maya refugee community through their experiences. The Reverend Frank O'Loughlin, Juan de la Calle, Joan Gannon, and Kathy Komarek of the Catholic Church in Indiantown have been important allies in the work. Research in Indiantown has been carried out with the generous hospitality of the Holy Cross Service Center and the help of many individuals in the community.

Support for the research that forms the basis of this book came from the U.S. Department of Labor, Immigration Policy Group; the University of Florida Division of Sponsored Research; the First Asylum Committee of the World Lutheran Church; the Presbyterian Women's Thank Offering; and the Southeast Florida March of Dimes Birth Defects Foundation.

Many of the ideas in this book were first presented at meetings of the Society for Applied Anthropology, American Anthropological Association, and Mesa Redonda de la Sociedad de Estudios Mayas de España, as well as in talks with colleagues in anthropology and linguistics. Some of the early pages of Chapter Three first appeared in my article "The Maya of Florida," *Migration World* 17, no. 3/4 (1989). Some of the material in Chapter Six first appeared in my essay "Internal and External Identity among Kanjobal Mayan Refugees in Florida," in *Conflict, Migration, and the Expression of Ethnicity*, ed. Nancie L. Gonzalez and Carolyn S. McCommon (Boulder: Westview Press, 1988).

Good discussions about the Maya of the United States and their traditional homeland came from many colleagues, including Alicia Re Cruz, Miguel Rivera Dorado, Nancie Gonzalez, Carolyn McCommon, Mary Elmendorf, Grant Jones, David Bolles, Barbara Pfeiler, Chris Lutz, Duncan Earl, James Loucky, Sandy Davis, Brian Page, Victor Montejo, and Murdo MacLeod. Barbara and Dennis Tedlock convinced me early on that scholarship demands both dedication and commitment; my orientation toward text, dialogue, and interpretation owes much to their clear writing on the subject. The applied work and human rights orientation of Paul and Polly Doughty has taught me that such work should be encouraged in both our private and our public lives. Colleagues at the University of Florida, including Terry McCoy, Helen Safa, Hernan Vera, Glaucio Soares, Steve Sanderson, Kent Redford, Anthony Oliver-Smith, and George Armelagos, have made working on this topic a pleasure. Elizabeth Eddy brought me to Florida from Arizona, and my own journey from Agua Prieta to Gainesville is due to her interest. Francisco Fernandez Repeto helped interview and make arrangements in the Quetzal Edzna refugee camp in Campeche, Mexico. Francisco Fernandez's and Genny Negroe's insights into everyday cultural resistance of the Maya of the Yucatan have been important to my understanding of the Maya way of life in Florida. Thanks also go to colleagues at the University of Copenhagen, where I was given the time and encouragement to complete the final editing of the book while on a Fulbright teaching exchange from 1991 to 1992.

My first teacher of Maya, Alonzo Gonzalez Mo, has died, but he sparked an interest in Maya thought that burns as bright today as it did twenty years ago. My *compadres* Luis Fernando Tuyub, Julia Martin Tuyub, and Mario Tuyub and his wife, Manuela, along with doña Seferiña Orozco de Tuyub and my *ahijados*, make understanding this new world worthwhile. Carlos Viera, Carlos Encalada, Alicia Gonzalez, and others at the Universidad Autónoma de Yucatán also deserve thanks for their friendship.

Julie Gray Burns stood close during these times and understood the distractions, the inconveniences, the pressing crises, and the occasional humor of my work.

Finally, I would like to thank Doris Braendel of Temple University Press, who encouraged me to put all of this in one book and whose editorial and conceptual skills helped to bring out this story and make it readable.

INTRODUCTION
Jerónimo Camposeco

PARA HABLAR SOBRE los exilados Mayas en Estados Unidos, necesito revelar algo de mi propia biografía donde se verá que mi existencia está estrechamente relacionada con los kanjobales, especialmente con los de San Miguel Acatán, quienes fueron los primeros inmigrantes al comienzo de la década de los ochenta. También quiero mencionar en este relato que sus habitantes y los de San Rafael La Independencia, en el departamento de Huehuetenango, Guatemala, son hablantes de kanjobal, aunque últimamente los lingüistas decidieron que este idioma se llame Akateko. Ellos tienen buenas razones científicas y no quiero contradecirles, pero por razones prácticas ese primer grupo de refugiados se les llamo kanjobales, como fue establecido en esa época y como eran conocidos y llamados por la sociedad norteamericana que los recibió.

Mis padres, José y Antonia, eran indígenas campesinos de Jacaltenango, un pueblo al noroeste de Huehuetenango, a quince kilómetros de San Miguel Acatán, los dos pueblos separados por las montañas Cuchumatecas y tres ríos. Mis padres tenían una tienda en el centro del pueblo, donde vendían víveres, ropa, y cortes típicos traídos de Salcajá, Quezaltenango. Mi mamá cosía ropa y hacía blusas para las mujeres jacaltecas en una máquina de coser de mano "Singer." Cuando era la fiesta anual del santo patronal de los pueblos circunvecinos, ellos cargaban una o dos mulas para llevar mercadería y vender en las plazas o mercados de cada uno de esos pueblos. En el lugar de esa venta provisional construían una especie de tienda de campaña con una manta blanca grande que llamábamos "manteado."

Era costumbre en los pueblos que esta celebración fuese la más importante del año, de modo que sus habitantes esperaban

IN ORDER TO TALK about the Mayan exiles in the United States, it is necessary to reveal something of my own biography. My personal history is closely related to that of the Kanjobal Maya, especially those of San Miguel Acatán, who were the first to immigrate to the United States at the beginning of the 1980s. In this context, I would also like to mention that the people of San Miguel and those of San Rafael La Independencia in the department of Huehuetenango, Guatemala, are Kanjobal Maya speakers, even though recently linguists have decided that this language should be called Akateko. The linguists have good, scientific reasons for this, and I do not want to contradict them, but for practical reasons this work refers to the first group of refugees as "Kanjobal." This term was the accepted one when these refugees arrived in the United States, and it is the one by which they are now known in the North American society that has received them.

My parents, José and Antonia, were indigenous *campesinos* of Jacaltenango, a town in the northwest of Huehuetenango. Jacaltenango is some fifteen kilometers from San Miguel Acatán and is separated from it by the Cuchumatan Mountains and three rivers. My parents had a store in the center of town where they sold supplies, clothes, and typical skirts brought from Salcajá, Quezaltenango. My mother was a seamstress and made blouses for the Jacaltec women on an old manual Singer sewing machine. When the annual patronal fiesta of the towns around us was held, my parents loaded up a mule or two to carry the merchandise and sell it in the plazas and markets of the towns. In each of these temporary locations they built a kind of store or stall with a big white canopy that we called a *manteado*.

con mucho entusiasmo la fiesta, en la cual trataban de "estrenar" ropa nueva, asistir a los actos religiosos, participar en la "cohetería" durante la noche principal de la celebración, ver o participar en los bailes tradicionales como el del venado, el de los Moros, o el de la conquista. Las plazas y hasta las calles se llenaban de "manteados" y "chinamas" (puestos de ventas de ramas de árboles). Como yo era el más pequeño de siete hermanos que éramos en la familia de tres hombres y cuatro mujeres, acompañaba siempre a mis padres a todas estas fiestas, algo que disfrutaba mucho porque conocía otros lugares y otras gentes y jugaba con nuevos amigos, a veces de diferentes lenguas y costumbres. Ya era una tradición para nosotros viajar cada año a las tierras altas y frías de Concepción Huista en la primera semana de diciembre, a San Marcos Huista a finales de abril, y el Cuarto Viernes de Cuaresma a Santa Ana Huista, lugar bajo, donde hace mucho calor pero donde gozaba bañándome en las aguas azules del profundo y ancho Río Huista, cuya ribera estaba cubierta de enormes árboles llamados "sabinos." Santa Ana es un lugar muy importante dentro de la tradición católica, porque en el Cuarto Viernes, llegan "romeristas" y peregrinos de todas partes y de diferentes culturas, incluyendo mexicanos, quienes llegaban caminando a veces de rodillas en grupos de promesas al santo "Jesús Nazareno" de Santa Ana. Era muy agradable ver a tanta gente con sus diferentes trajes típicos, costumbres, música, y bailes. Aquí conocí por primera vez el "mariachi mexicano." Sin embargo, ir a la fiesta de San Miguel en los últimos días de septiembre era para nosotros algo diferente, algo familiar y más propio.

Era muy difícil llegar a San Miguel, porque se caminaba a pie o a caballo en los días más lluviosos del año. En consecuencia, los caminos estaban muy lodosos, difíciles de transitar; además había que subir y bajar cerros muy empinados, cruzando muchos arroyos y ríos. Pero estos sacrificios e in-

It was the custom in those towns that the patronal celebration was the most important event of the year, and consequently the people awaited the fiesta with great enthusiasm.
They brought out the best of their new clothes, participated in
religious activities, and watched the fireworks during the main
night of the celebration. They also attended and participated in
traditional dances like the Dance of the Deer, the Dance of the
Moros, and the Dance of the Conquest. The plazas and even the
streets around them were filled with covered stalls and *chinamas* (market stalls made of the branches of trees). As the youngest of seven children (we were a family of three boys and four
girls), I always accompanied my parents to these fiestas. It was
something that I enjoyed very much because I was able to visit
other places and other people and to play with new friends, even
ones who spoke different languages and had different customs.
It was a tradition for us to travel each year to the high, cold lands
of Concepción Huista during the first week of December and to
San Marcos Huista at the end of April, and to Santa Ana Huista
during the four Fridays of Lent. Santa Ana Huista was a place in
the lowlands where it was very hot but where I liked to swim in
the deep blue waters of the Rio Huista. The riverbank was
covered with enormous trees that were called *sabinos.* Santa
Ana is a very important place in the Catholic tradition, because
during the four Fridays of Lent pilgrims and other travelers
arrive from all over. Even Mexicans walk to the site, sometimes
in groups on their knees as a promise to Jesus of Nazareth of
Santa Ana. It was always marvelous to see so many people with
their different costumes, customs, music, and dances. This is
where I first heard a Mexican mariachi band.

Each year we went to the fiesta of San Miguel at the end of
September. The fiesta of San Miguel was something different for
us, something more familiar and more our own. It was very
difficult to get to San Miguel, because you had to walk or ride a

comodidades no eran un gran obstáculo, porque estos viajes tenían una gran importancia para nosotros por su significado religioso profundo, por costumbre, y porque constituían nuestro "modus vivendi," en vista de que nuestra vida así como la de todos los indígenas de esa región estaba supeditada a una "estricta economía de subsistencia."

He ahí que mis padres no podían faltar a la fiesta de San Miguel en septiembre de 1939, a pesar de que mi madre estaba muy indispuesta porque estaba en un grado muy avanzado de embarazo, esperándome a mí. El "mero" día de la fiesta era el 29. Sin embargo, mi mamá de repente se sintió muy mal ya con síntomas de darme a luz un día antes. Entonces ellos se alarmaron tanto que decidieron regresar a Jacaltenango, puesto que en San Miguel no había doctor ni clínica y no conocían a una comadrona de confianza, sólo a la que conocían en nuestro pueblo por muchos años. Estando allí, ellos ya me habían asignado el nombre de Miguel, porque el 29, el día del santo, iba a ser el gran día. No fue así, sino hasta el 30 de septiembre de 1939, el día de San Jerónimo; he allí mi nombre de pila.

Contentos mis papás, respetando la tradición, llamaron a los "Alcaldes Rezadores" o "Alcal Txah" (sacerdotes mayas), para que fueran a rezar y quemar "copal" en mi casa y en los cerros sagrados del pueblo.

Como mi papá estaba muy ocupado, no fue a la Municipalidad hasta el otro día a asentar mi nombre. Pero por razones hasta ahora incomprendidas, el día de mi nacimiento fue inscrito oficialmente el primero de octubre de 1938, exactamente un día después y un año antes de mi natalicio.

Como se podrá observar, por un azar del destino mi relación comienza con el pueblo y la gente de San Miguel Acatán desde el día de mi nacimiento, tanto que por poco nazco en el "mero" pueblo para convertirme físicamente en un migueleno auténtico. Sin embargo, moral, sentimental y solidariamente sí lo soy.

horse during the rainiest days of the year. The roads were, as a consequence, very muddy and difficult to travel. Besides, you had to climb up and down over hills that were very steep and cross many arroyos and rivers. But these sacrifices and inconveniences were not great obstacles, because the trips to San Miguel were so important to us. The fiesta had deep religious significance, it was our family custom, and it constituted our way of life, as it did for all the indigenous people of the region. We were united by the fiesta and also because we shared a strict subsistence economy.

So it was that my parents felt they could not miss the fiesta of San Miguel in September of 1939, even though my mother was indisposed since she was about to give birth to me. The day of the fiesta was the 29th, and my mother felt very bad by then, since she had begun labor the day before. My parents became so alarmed that they decided to go back to Jacaltenango, since in San Miguel there was neither a doctor nor a clinic. Besides, they did not know any midwives, as they did in our town, where they had lived for many years. If I had been born in San Miguel, I would have been named Miguel, because the 29th is the day of that saint, and it would have been a great day to be born. I was not born, though, until September 30, 1939, the day of San Jerónimo. As is customary, Jerónimo became my baptismal name.

My parents were people who respected Maya tradition. When I was born, they called the "prayer specialists," or Alcal Txah (the Maya priests), so that they could pray and burn *copal* incense in my house and in the sacred hills of the town. My father was so busy that he waited a few days to go to the municipal center to fill out my birth certificate. But for reasons I still do not understand, my birthday was officially recorded as October 1, 1938, exactly one day after and one year before my birth.

And so by a chance of fate, my relationship with the town

Pasaron los años; la vida en Jacaltenango siguió su curso normal. Mi papá, con la ayuda de mis hermanos, cultivaba maíz, frijol, tomate, y café en unos pequeños sembrados que tenía en el pueblo y en la "tierra caliente" o tierras bajas cerca de la frontera con Chiapas. Mi mamá, además de los quehaceres del hogar se dedicaba a la tienda y a la costura. Pero a veces asistía a los niños enfermos y mujeres pobres, ya sea con alimentos o medicina natural; pues era considerada en el pueblo como una buena curandera de buenos sentimientos humanos. Pero un día, cuando yo apenas tenía siete años, desgraciadamente mi madre murió de una enfermedad repentina que la atacó después de haber regresado de misa. Su partida causó en todos nosotros un tremendo vacío y una gran pesadumbre difícil de describir. Los meses subsiguientes se convirtieron para nosotros en los más dificultosos y críticos. Yo tuve una niñez incompleta porque estudiaba la primaria cuando podía y trabajaba con mi papá en el campo o viajaba con él a vender a los pueblos junto con una de mis hermanas. La tragedia continuó en la familia cuando mi papá dispuso casarse no con una jacalteca sino con una "ladina," muy extraña para nosotros. No sólo su cultura era diferente sino que también tenía unas intenciones macabras: consumió y vendió todo lo de la tienda, derrochó sin conservar para el consumo los productos agrícolas, más nos supeditó a maltrato y discriminación.

Mis hermanos, como ya eran grandes, dispusieron separarse y casarse huyendo de la pesadilla que se vivía en el nuevo hogar. Yo en cambio me quedé viviendo ese infierno y trabajando fuertemente en el campo para satisfacer las necesidades de la nueva familia de mi padre que cada vez iba creciendo. Fueron tan grandes esas necesidades que los terrenos que mis padres habían obtenido con tanto sacrificio, la nueva señora de Camposeco, sin embargo, los iba vendiendo poco a poco hasta llevarnos a la bancarrota. Naturalmente la tienda desapareció y todos quedamos sumergidos en el nivel más extremo de pobreza.

and people of San Miguel Acatán began with the day of my birth, so much so that I almost was actually born in the town, which would have physically made me an authentic child of San Miguel. Even so, I am a child of San Miguel in moral and sentimental terms as well as in terms of the solidarity I feel with the people.

Life in Jacaltenango continued on a normal course as the years passed. With the help of my brothers, my father planted corn, beans, tomatoes, and coffee in the small fields that he had in the town and in the *tierra caliente* (hot lands), the lowlands near the border with Chiapas. My mother, in addition to doing the housework, devoted her time to the store and worked as a seamstress. At times she would also help sick children and poor women, either with food or with natural medicine. In the town she was considered a good health practitioner (or "curer") with a good heart.

Unfortunately, one day when I was just seven years old, my mother died of a sudden illness that overcame her when she returned from mass. Her death created a tremendous emptiness in our lives and a deep depression that is difficult to describe. The next several months were very difficult and critical for us. I had an incomplete childhood because I went to elementary school when I could and then worked with my father in the fields or traveled with him to sell things in the towns along with one of my sisters. The tragedy continued within the family when my father later married a *ladina* rather than a Jacaltecan woman, which was very unusual for us. Not only were her customs and culture different but she also had evil intentions. She consumed and sold everything in the store, squandering it without saving any of the agricultural products, and abused and mistreated us as well.

My brothers and sisters were already grown, and so they married and left, to escape the misfortune that now filled our home. On the other hand, I continued to live in this hell and

En los años de bonanza, me gustaba particularmente trabajar con mi papá en un lugar de tierra fría llamado "Huitzobal" arriba de la aldea San Marcos Huista, camino a San Miguel, casi en la punta de un cerro. Nos quedábamos a dormir en una casa rústica de palos y techo de paja de una familia miguelena cuyos miembros eran amigos nuestros. Nos acostábamos en el suelo junto al fuego de leña, para no sentir frío en las noches. El jefe de familia se llamaba "Shunic," su esposa "Malin," sus hijas "Lolen" y "Ashul," y sus hijos "Cashin" y "Mekel." Estos jóvenes en esa época tenían dieciocho, dieciseis, catorce, y doce años respectivamente. Era increíble el buen trato y la atención que estos amables miguelenos nos brindaban, sobre todo la comida "vegetariana" que consistía en una sopa de punta de "chilacayote" (hojas, flores y frutos tiernos de una especie de calabaza de tierra fría), ejotes verdes, elotes, papas criollas, y aguacate, todo cosechado naturalmente en los alrededores de la casa que estaba en medio de la milpa.

Mi papá había permitido a Shunic vivir con su familia en sus tierras y sembrar milpa junto a la de nosotros. El mejor tiempo con ellos era en tiempo de cosecha; las mazorcas de maíz las guardábamos en las "trojas" (unas casas pequeñas de troncos y paja). La razón de meter el maíz allí era que el clima frío protegía por más tiempo las mazorcas de los "gorgojos" (insectos voraces que destruyen el maíz). En Jacaltenango o en las tierras bajas donde el clima es templado o cálido, estos gorgojos abundaban, tanto que en poco tiempo arruinan el maíz que se guarda para el consumo.

La comunicación entre miguelenos y jacaltecos es muy fácil ya que el jacalteco, el kanjobal, y akateco son muy similares. En tiempos antiguos, Jacaltenango era considerado un centro muy importante para los pueblos indígenas vecinos. Culturalmente los miguelenos estaban relacionados con ese pueblo, pero también económicamente. Aún recuerdo que en los fines de semana

worked hard in the fields to meet the needs of my father's new family, which continued to grow. These needs were so great that the lands that my parents had obtained at considerable sacrifice were sold off one by one by the new Mrs. Camposeco until we were bankrupt. Naturally, the store disappeared, and we all descended to the most extreme level of poverty.

During the good years, I particularly liked to work with my father in a place in the "cold lands" called Huitzobal, which was above the hamlet of San Marcos Huista on the San Miguel road. It was right at the tree line. We would stay there and sleep in a thatched-roofed wooden cottage that belonged to a family from San Miguel who were friends of ours. We would sleep on the floor next to the wood fire so that we wouldn't be cold at night. The head of the family was called Shunic, his wife was Malin, the daughters were Lolen and Ashul, and the sons were called Cashin and Mekel. At that time these youngsters were eighteen, sixteen, fourteen, and twelve years old, respectively. The good will and attention that these friendly Miguelenos gave us was incredible. Best of all was the "vegetarian" food, which consisted of chilacayote soup (leaves, flowers, and tender squash from the "cold lands"), green beans, green corn, "creole"-style potatoes, and avocado. All was grown naturally in the area around the house, which was in the middle of the cornfield.

My father had given Shunic permission to live with his family and cultivate his cornfield, or *milpa*, in the lands next to ours. Most of the time during harvest season we stored our own corn with theirs in the *trojas* (small houses made of sticks and thatch). The reason we kept the corn there was that the cold protected the corn for a long time from the weevils that were so plentiful in Jacaltenango and the lowlands, where the climate is more temperate or hot and corn that is stored for eating is quickly ruined.

Communication between Miguelenos and Jacaltecos is very

ellos bajaban de sus montañas a vender diferentes productos tales como las vigas hormigones para construcción de casas de pino o pinabete. La forma de cargarlas era una tarea pesada y complicada. En cada viaje traían dos: un hombre se ponía en medio pero en un extremo, y otro hombre cargaba de la misma forma en el otro extremo. De ese modo las vigas de diez metros de largo con un peso de ochenta a cien libras cada una eran transportadas a Jacaltenango por esos campesinos, caminando dificultosamente uno enfrente del otro por esos angostos y empinados senderos de las montañas. Otros miguelenos llevaban tablas de madera para muebles, ventanas, o puertas. También iban a vender un pan especial que llamamos "sheca," hecho de trigo café no refinado, pero de un sabor delicioso. Otros artículos de mucha demanda eran los productos de fibra de maguey (ishte) tales como cuerdas, "lazos," "jaquimas" para atar bestias, "morrales" (bolsas), redes, adornos de pared, etcétera. Asimismo fabricaban artículos de lana de oveja negra, como los sacos cerrados o "capishayes" para protegerse del frío o la lluvia, los manteones para los aparejos o monturas de caballos. Las mujeres especializaron en tejer una cinta de palma al que llamamos "trenza" para la fábrica de sombreros en Jacaltenango y sobre todo para los sombreros especiales que usan los mames de Todos Santos. De esta forma podían sobrevivir los miguelenos, porque la tierra de su municipio no produce lo suficiente porque es de mala calidad y está en las laderas de la montaña donde la erosión constante ha convertido los terrenos prácticamente en inservibles. Es ésta una de las razones por la cual los miguelenos son una población constantemente móvil y migrante.

Es común en Guatemala y en Chiapas encontrar en las fincas de café, algodón, cardamomo, y caña de azúcar a miguelenos con sus familias trabajando por un bajo salario, expuestos a mal trato, al sol ardiente, a los pesticidas, y a enfermedades tropicales de malaria y disentería.

easy, since Jacaltec, Kanjobal, and Acatec are very similar dialects. In the old times, Jacaltenango was considered an important center by the indigenous communities around it. The Miguelenos were related to the community culturally as well as economically. I remember that every weekend they would come down from the mountains to sell different things, such as the wooden beams used for building pine houses (*pinabete*). Carrying the beams to Jacaltenango was a cumbersome and complicated task. The *campesinos* carried two beams each trip: one man positioned himself between the poles at the front, and the other held the same position in the back. In this way, walking with great difficulty, one in front of the other on the narrow and rocky mountain trails, they carried beams over thirty feet long and weighing from eighty to one hundred pounds. Other Miguelenos brought boards for furniture or doors. They also sold a special kind of bread that we called *sheca*. It was made of unrefined dark wheat and had a delicious flavor. Other items that were very popular were items made of maguey fiber (*ishte*) like rope, lassos, harnesses for animals, *morrales*, or sacks, nets, wall hangings, and so forth. They also made articles from black wool, such as ponchos, or *capishayes*, to protect people from the cold or rain, and saddle blankets for horses. The women were specialists in weaving a sash of palm that we called *trenza*, which was used to make hats in Jacaltenango and especially those used by the Mam people of Todos Santos.

This is the way the Miguelenos survived, because the lands of their district could not produce enough. The lands were of poor quality and situated on the hillsides, where constant erosion had made them practically useless. This, then, is one of the reasons why the Miguelenos are a people who migrate and move often. It is common to find large plantations of coffee, cotton, cardamom, and sugar cane in Guatemala and Chiapas, where Miguelenos work with their families for low wages, ex-

El tiempo pasó; finalmente pude liberarme del problema del hogar de mi padre. Cuando tenía quince años le pedí ayuda al sacerdote Maryknoll de mi pueblo, para que me apoyara y me mandara a estudiar al seminario en Quezaltenango, junto con otros jóvenes jacaltecos que habían sido seleccionados previamente. El padre aceptó gustosamente, pero a mi papá no le gustó la idea, porque con mi partida se quedaba solo en el trabajo pesado del campo para sostener a su familia. No contaba con la ayuda de sus hijos que ya tenía, porque eran muy pequeños todavía.

Viendo esta situación, el sacerdote llamó a mi papá a su oficina para hablar con él, donde lo convenció para que me permitiera viajar, argumentando que no se opusiera a mi "vocación." Como buen católico debía aceptar y respetar mi decisión. Es posible que faltara a la honestidad tratando de manipular al sacerdote; sin embargo, la vida de estudio en el seminario me atraía bastante y realmente así fue en los cinco años que estuve allí. Después me salí, pero por otras razones que no vienen al caso contar. Continué viviendo en Quezaltenango en casa de una familia que había conocido durante mis años de estudio, porque el más joven de sus miembros también estaba estudiando en el seminario.

Después de haber luchado bastante, finalmente pude conseguir trabajo en la Casa de la Cultura de Quezaltenango, atendiendo la librería. Quizás apenas tenía un mes de estar allí cuando un día de febrero de 1960, durante la mañana, un venerable hombre entró y se dirigió a donde yo estaba y me dijo, "Hola, Jerónimo. ¿Cómo estás? ¿Te acuerdas? Soy el Padre Jaime Curtin." Yo reaccioné, recordé, y le contesté, "Claro que sí lo recuerdo; usted fue párroco en Jacaltenango hace muchos años." "Sí, es cierto," me dijo. "Ahora estoy en San Miguel Acatán. Supe que no estabas ya en el seminario; por eso te vine a buscar para pedirte que te fueras conmigo a San Miguel a trabajar en la

posed to abuse, the hot sun, pesticides, and tropical illnesses such as dysentery and malaria.

The time passed, and I was finally able to free myself from the problem of my father's household. When I was fifteen, I asked a Maryknoll priest from my community to help me by sending me to study at the seminary in Quezaltenango along with other Jacaltecan boys who had already been selected. The priest readily agreed, but my father didn't like the idea because if I left, he would have to do the hard work in the fields by himself to sustain his family. He could not count on the help of his new children, since they were still very young.

The priest reviewed this situation and called my father into his office, where he convinced him to let me go, arguing that my father should not, as a good Catholic, oppose my "vocation" but should accept and respect my decision. Now it is possible that I manipulated the priest. At the time, however, I was really attracted to the life of study in the seminary; it remained that way for the five years that I was there, but eventually I left for other, unrelated reasons.

After leaving the seminary, I continued to live in Quezaltenango in the house of a family that I had gotten to know during my years of study, since their youngest had also studied in the seminary. After much hard work, I was finally able to get a job in the Casa de la Cultura de Quezaltenango, working in the library. I had been there about a month when one day during February 1960, in the morning, an older man entered and came toward me. He said, "Hello, Jerónimo. How are you? Do you remember? I am Father James."

I was struck, I remembered him, and I said, "Of course I remember you. You were the parish priest in Jacaltenango many years ago."

"Yes, you're right," he said. "Now I'm in San Miguel Acatán. I heard that you were no longer in the seminary, so I came to look

escuela de la parroquia como maestro. ¿Aceptas?" Bastante sorprendido, me quedé pensando un momento en lo que parecía una buena idea, trabajar entre gente de mi propia cultura. Pero por otro lado quería quedarme en Quezaltenango para seguir estudiando en las noches. Pero en verdad en ese momento tenía grandes problemas económicos y viendo la oferta del padre, podría en corto tiempo resolver en gran parte ese problema, de modo que le contesté diciendo, "Sí, Padre, acepto."

San Miguel estaba muy lejos, como a un día en carro. Teníamos que subir completamente los montes Cuchumatanes y luego bajar por una gran pendiente para llegar al pueblo prácticamente al otro lado de la montaña. Cuando llegué a San Miguel, también a mi mente llegaron agradables recuerdos de mi niñez cuando solíamos venir aquí en la fiesta con mis padres todos los años. Encontré en la escuela parroquial muchos niños kanjobales no sólo del pueblo sino también de las aldeas. Los padres tenían allí mismo un internado para los niños aldeanos. El colegio tenía hasta quinto grado de primaria, pero había un grado pre-escolar llamado "Castellanización," un programa creado por el gobierno para enseñar a los niños indígenas monolingües el español de modo que puedan entender al maestro en las clases de primaria que eran en castellano. Habían dos religiosas de la orden de Maryknoll que manejaban el colegio. Nostros éramos cinco maestros indígenas de diferentes pueblos: dos jacaltecos que éramos Ramón Lino y yo; Santiago Ben y José Aguirre, de San Miguel; y Diego Juan, de Santa Eulalia. A mí me asignaron la clase de castellanización; algunos de esos alumnos mios están grandes con familia y viven ahora en Indiantown, Fort Myers, y Los Angeles.

Como era un colegio católico, había que observar un reglamento religioso bastante estricto de acuerdo a la moral cristiana, pero también había que respetar la cultura y las costumbres de los miguelenos.

for you to ask if you would come with me to San Miguel and work in the parish school as a teacher. Do you want to?"

Completely surprised, I stood there a minute, thinking that it seemed like a good idea to work among people of my own culture but that, on the other hand, I wanted to stay in Quezaltenango to continue studying at night. But I had serious financial problems at this time, and I realized that the priest's offer would allow me to solve them in a short time. So I responded, "Yes, Father, I accept the position."

San Miguel was far away—a day's drive by car. We had to go all the way up the Cuchumatan Mountains and then down a long way to arrive at the town, which was practically on the other side of the mountains. The town brought back fond memories of my childhood, of all the years when we had come to San Miguel for the fiesta with my parents.

In the parish school I found many Kanjobal children not only from the town but also from the villages. The priests had built a boarding house for the village children. The school went up to the fifth grade of primary school but had one year of preschool called "Castellanización," a program created by the government to teach Spanish to monolingual indigenous children so that they could understand the teachers in the primary school classes, which were taught in Spanish. Two sisters from the Maryknoll order ran the school. There were also five indigenous teachers from different towns: two Jacaltecos (Ramón Lino and I), Santiago Ben and José Aguirre from San Miguel, and Diego Juan from Santa Eulalia. I was assigned to teach Spanish. Some of my students from those days, now adults with families, live today in Indiantown, Fort Myers, and Los Angeles.

Since the school was Catholic, we were expected to observe religious rules that were quite strict and in accordance with Christian morals. But we were also expected to respect the culture and customs of the people of San Miguel.

Cabe explicar que este tipo de escuela era reciente en San Miguel; las escuelas públicas eran muy escasas y no cubrían las necesidades educativas de la población rural, cosa muy común en Guatemala y en todos los países del tercer mundo. Los Maryknoll vieron esa necesidad; entonces decidieron crear escuelas gratuitas en cada una de sus parroquias en todo el departamento. Cuando las monjas religiosas fueron a las aldeas a reclutar niños para el colegio, se encontraron con el fenómeno social que también los adultos eran todos analfabetas; por tal motivo ellas decidieron enrolar en la escuela a jóvenes adolescentes también. Por eso en las clases regulares estaban revueltos los adolescentes y los niños.

En el pueblo tenía una amiga de origen mexicano. Su nombre era Cristabel Córdoba. Tenía dos niños de edad escolar, Mario y Jorge. Eramos muy buenos amigos. Ella atendía el puesto de salud local. Durante nuestros tiempos libres nos visitábamos, paseábamos juntos, y charlábamos sobre nuestras vidas con confianza. Como yo estaba solo, ella me daba de comer y me lavaba y planchaba la ropa sin cobrarme un centavo; trataba de pagarle o pedirle que no lo hiciera, pero ella insistía en servirme gustosamente. La noche antes de salir de San Miguel con Ramón, uno de mis compañeros de trabajo, fui a visitar a Cristabel para contarle lo de mi partida al siguiente día. Ella y sus niños se entristecieron profundamente, tanto que Cristabel se puso a llorar. No nos quedó más que consolarnos, prometiéndonos mutua solidaridad y una constante comunicación por correo en vista de que sería difícil volvernos a ver. Al otro día como a las cinco de la mañana, Ramón y yo salimos caminando cargando nuestras maletas rumbo a Villa Linda, un lugar cerca de la cumbre, como a doce kilómetros de distancia, de donde saldría un bus de pasajeros a la ciudad de Huehuetenango a las ocho de la mañana. ¡Cuál fue nuestra sorpresa que Cristabel y sus hijos nos estaban esperando en la orilla del pueblo para acompañar-

I have to explain that this kind of school was a recent addition to San Miguel. Public schools were rare and did not meet the educational needs of the rural population, as is very common in Guatemala and in all of the countries of the third world. The Maryknoll sisters saw this lack and decided to create free schools in each of their parishes throughout the department of Huehuetenango. When the nuns went to the villages to recruit children for the school, they discovered that adults were also illiterate. For that reason, they decided to allow teenagers to enroll in the school as well. The regular classes consisted of adolescents and children together.

In town I had a Mexican friend whose name was Cristabel Córdoba. She had two school-aged children, Mario and Jorge. Cristabel and I were good friends. She had a job in the local health unit, and during our free time we would visit, passing the hours together comfortably and talking about our lives. Since I was alone, she fed me and washed and ironed my clothes without charging me a penny. When I tried to pay her and asked her not to do these things, she insisted that helping me was a pleasure.

The night before I left San Miguel with Ramón, one of my co-workers, I went to explain to Cristabel that I was leaving the next day. She and her children were very upset; Cristabel even began to cry. We stayed only long enough to console each other, promising to remain friends and to write to one another, since it would be difficult for us to see each other again.

The next day at five o'clock in the morning, Ramón and I left by foot, carrying our bags on the way to Villa Linda, a place close to the summit, about twelve kilometers away, from which a bus would leave for the city of Huehuetenango at eight o'clock in the morning. Imagine our surprise when we found Cristabel and her children waiting for us at the edge of town to accompany us. "Doña Cristabel, you are so wonderful and I very much appreci-

nos! "Doña Cristabel, es usted muy amable y agradezco mucho su actitud, pero no quiero que usted y los niños se sacrifiquen por acompañarnos hasta Villa Linda. Vea que es una cuesta pedregosa y larga; por favor no vayan," le supliqué. "No," dijo, "yo voy con ustedes; pues quiero que sepa cuanto lo estimamos y sentimos mucho su partida. Permita demostrarle mi gran aprecio por usted acompañándolos hasta el bus." "Está bien," le dije, "y muchísimas gracias."

A pesar del frío de la mañana, la empinada y pedregosa cuesta nos hizo sudar y tomar intervalos de tiempo para descansar. Llegamos como media hora antes de la partida del bus, lo que aprovechamos para desayunar, descansar, y charlar un rato. El momento de salir llegó, y con un abrazo fuerte de despedida le dije adiós a Cristabel y a sus niños visiblemente entristecidos. Ya en el bus, mientras subíamos la carretera de tierra y piedras lentamente, yo iba pensando y meditando en San Miguel y su gente. Pero poniendo atención a la realidad del momento, ví allá abajo que los brazos de tres amigos queridos nos estaban diciendo adiós para siempre. Como habíamos quedado, Ramón se fue a la Zona Militar del Quiche, yo a Quezaltenango, donde pronto encontré trabajo en un hotel. Luego con mucho sacrificio continué mis estudios hasta lograr graduarme de maestro de escuela después de tres años de lucha. De ahí me fuí a la ciudad de Guatemala donde empecé a trabajar en el Instituto Indigenista Nacional durante catorce años. Tuve la oportunidad de estudiar antropología social en la Universidad de San Carlos. Pero por la violencia y persecución que sufrí de parte de grupos paramilitares asociados con el gobierno, tuve que salir huyendo para Estados Unidos con mi esposa y cuatro niños para salvar nuestras vidas.

Cuando aún estaba en Guatemala, las noticias anunciaron una gran Marcha de Mineros que venían desde Huehuetenango a la capital en el mes de noviembre de 1977. Esta marcha co-

ate your presence, but I don't want you and your children to make the sacrifice of coming with us to Villa Linda. You know that the way is rocky and long. Please don't come along," I begged.

"No," she said, "I'm going with you because I want you to know how much you mean to us and how bad we feel about your leaving. Let me show you my great esteem for you by coming with you to the bus."

"OK," I said, "and thank you so much."

In spite of the cold of the morning, the steep and rocky route made us sweat, and we had to take time to rest. We got to the bus stop about half an hour before the bus left, and we used that time to eat, rest, and talk a little. The moment to leave came, and we hugged Cristabel and her children good-bye. They were visibly moved. As I sat in the bus while we were still on the unpaved road, I thought about San Miguel and its people. But when I turned my attention to the reality of the present moment, I saw the waving arms of those three dear friends, who were saying good-bye forever.

Ramón went to the Military Zone of El Quiche, and I went to Quezaltenango, where I soon found work in a hotel. Later, with a lot of effort, I continued my studies and finally graduated as a schoolteacher after three years of struggle. From Quezaltenango I went to Guatemala City, where I worked with the National Indigenous Institute for fourteen years. There I had the opportunity to study social anthropology at the University of San Carlos. But because of the violence and persecution that I suffered from paramilitary groups associated with the government, I had to escape to the United States with my wife and four children in order to spare our lives.

When I was still in Guatemala, news reports announced that there would be a big Miners March from Huehuetenango to the capital in November 1977. This march began in the village of

menzó en el pueblo de Ixtahuacan por unos mineros de origen indígena en un recorrido de trescientos kilómetros a pie hasta la Capital, como protesta por el maltrato, explotación, y discriminación que sufrían en la compañía minera. Esta marcha la hicieron como último recurso para pedirle al gobierno su intervención y resolver este problema laboral. Las autoridades locales nunca escucharon estos clamores de justicia por la presión de los militares y los ejecutivos de la compañía.

También las noticias dijeron que el organizador de esta marcha era Mario Mujia Córdoba (Wiwi), el hijo de Cristabel Córdoba, mi amiga enfermera de San Miguel Acatán. Desgraciadamente el gobierno militar no resolvió el problema de los mineros.

Mario siguió luchando a favor de los campesinos y obreros de esa región, pero el día 20 de julio de 1978, estando él en su oficina de ayuda legal para los pobres que recientemente había fundado, hombres desconocidos fuertemente armados lo asesinaron cobardemente con ráfagas de ametralladora.

Pero ésta tragedia aumentó en su sufrida familia; días después su hermano Jorge (quien trabajaba como locutor en la Radio Nuevo Mundo de la capital) fue secuestrado, también por hombres desconocidos, y seguramente asesinado, porque jamás volvió a aparecer. Los asesinos no descansaron, y siguieron llevando el dolor a esa familia; la hija menor de Cristabel, quien ya era una señorita pero que no pude conocer en San Miguel en 1960, fue también secuestrada, torturada, violada, y muerta, por el mismo tipo de hombres que mataron a sus hermanos. Se tienen pruebas que los militares de la Base Armada de Huehuetenango cometían estos crímenes impunemente, vestidos de particular.

Cristabel, una heroína, una madre valiente y amorosa, con un corazón tremendamente humano y un alma sensitiva, ha de haber sufrido estas pérdidas lamentables de sus queridos hijos

Ixtahuacan among a few indigenous miners, who journeyed three hundred kilometers to the capital as a protest against the mistreatment, exploitation, and discrimination they suffered at the hands of the mining company. The march was a last resort to petition the national government to intervene and resolve the labor problems. The local authorities never listened to these calls for justice because of pressure from the military and from company executives. The news reports also said that the organizer of the march was Mario Mujía Córdoba (Wiwi), the son of Cristabel Córdoba, my friend the nurse from San Miguel Acatán.

The military government unfortunately did not resolve the miners' problems. Mario continued to struggle for the good of the *campesinos* and workers of the region, but on July 20, 1978, in the office that he had recently opened to provide legal help for the poor, some unknown armed men assassinated him with a burst of machine-gun fire.

More suffering for the family was added to this tragedy. Days later Mario's brother Jorge (who worked as an announcer at Radio Nuevo Mundo in the capital) was kidnapped, also by unknown men, and was surely assassinated, because he never reappeared. The assassins did not rest. They continued to bring pain to this family. Cristabel's youngest daughter, who was at this time a young woman and whom I had not known in San Miguel in 1960, was also kidnapped, tortured, raped, and killed by the same sorts of men who had killed her brothers. There is proof that the soldiers of the Base Armada de Huehuetenango committed these crimes with impunity, dressed as private citizens.

Cristabel was a heroine, a valiant mother with great love, a tremendously humane heart, and a sensitive spirit. Her suffering caused by the tragic loss of her dear children must have been indescribable. Unfortunately, I could never personally console

de una manera indescriptible. Desgraciadamente nunca pude consolarla personalmente, no sólo por la lejanía que nos separaba, sino porque también yo era un perseguido como lo fueron sus hijos.

Al comienzo de la década de los ochenta, la actitud paranoica del militarismo y de las fuerzas conservadoras, que esgrimieron excusas de seguridad nacional en vez de cuestionar las causas de las injusticias y la miseria de los guatemaltecos, resultó en una campaña macabra de muerte, destrucción, y exterminio nunca antes vista en los anales históricos de la nación. Me contaron que aquellos amigos miguelenos eran cogidos por los soldados cuando bajaban al día de mercado en Jacaltenango y, acusándolos de guerrilleros falsamente, los capturaban en el camino, los ataban a un árbol, y con la punta de una daga les martilleaban su frente, haciéndolos gritar del terrible dolor hasta desmayarse y morir. A otros los despojaban de sus cosas que llevaban a vender, y simplemente los mataban lentamente a machetazos, argumentando que no querían desperdiciar sus balas y municiones. Mucha gente inocente murió de diferentes formas en el municipio de San Miguel y San Rafael. Esa crueldad militar fue aplicada también en la mayoría de los pueblos indígenas de Guatemala. Cientos de miles logramos escapar, huyendo hacia México o a Estados Unidos, mortificados por el dolor, angustiados por nuestra sobrevivencia en tierras desconocidas, pero estimulados amargamente por la ira.

Yo me refugié en la granja de una comunidad nativa en Pennsylvania; gracias a la generosidad de sus miembros, sobre todo la de mi amigo Rarihokwats, y al apoyo de los grupos de solidaridad, pude iniciar una campaña política-educativa en forma de conferencias, enfatizando los mensajes con mi propio testimonio. Así fue como viajé a muchos lugares de Estados Unidos y Canadá, con presentaciones personales, a veces acompañado con música de marimba guatemalteca en vivo.

her, not only because of the distance that separated us but also because, like her children, I was being pursued.

At the beginning of the eighties, the paranoia of the military and conservative forces, who used national security as an excuse instead of addressing the causes of injustice and misery among Guatemalans, resulted in a macabre campaign of death, destruction, and extermination never before seen in the history of the nation. I was told that when my friends from San Miguel came down to Jacaltenango on market day, they were arrested by soldiers and falsely accused of being guerrillas. The soldiers captured them on the road, tied them to a tree, and with the point of a dagger repeatedly stabbed their foreheads, making them scream with agony until they lost consciousness and died. Others were stripped of the goods they had brought to sell and were slowly killed with machete blows, since the soldiers said that they did not want to waste their ammunition. Many innocent people died in different ways in the district of San Miguel and San Rafael. This military cruelty was also carried out in most of the indigenous communities of Guatemala. Hundreds of thousands of us were able to escape, fleeing into Mexico or the United States, humiliated by the pain, in anguish over how we would survive in unknown lands, but bitterly energized by our rage.

I became a refugee on a farm belonging to a Native American community in Pennsylvania. Thanks to the generosity and support of its members—above all, that of my friend Rarihokwats—I was able to begin a political and educational speaking tour, emphasizing my message with my own testimony. Traveling throughout the United States and Canada, I made many personal appearances, sometimes accompanied by live Guatemalan marimba music.

On one of my trips to an Indian nation in the north of New York state, I met the mother and sister of my Mohawk Indian

En uno de mis viajes a un territorio indígena en el norte del estado de Nueva York, conocí a la madre y a la hermana de mi amigo indio Mohawk, Kayuta Clouds, con quien había trabajado en Guatemala en un proyecto de agricultura orgánica y una escuela de cultura, ciencia y filosofía maya para los hermanos mayas cakchiqueles de Poaquil, Chimaltenango. Un día en octubre de 1980, después de sus clases, Kayuta fue al mercado a comprar su comida. Cuando regresó y pasó frente al parque de la ciudad de Chimaltenango, seis hombres fuertemente armados se le acercaron repentinamente, lo cogieron, lo golpearon, y lo metieron violentamente en un carro partiendo a un rumbo desconocido, frente a muchos testigos y agentes de la policía nacional que no hicieron nada para pararlos. Días más tarde su cadáver apareció brutalmente golpeado, con señales de tortura, abandonado en las calles de Antigua Guatemala. El rostro de la madre de Kay reflejaba un profundo sufrimiento. Aún así, me sonreía, me abrazaba, y me animaba, dándome fuerzas para luchar y denunciar las injusticias y sus verdaderas causas en nombre de su hijo que sacrificó su vida valiosa por la causa maya.

En febrero de 1983 los jefes Mohawk y los editores del periódico indio *Akwesasne Notes* me llamaron urgentemente, pidiéndome que los acompañara a la Florida para asistir a los abogados del Florida Rural Legal Services (FRLS) y del American Friends Service Committee (AFSC) que estaban defendiendo a unos kanjobales de San Miguel Acatán, detenidos en las cárceles del Immigration and Naturalization Service (Krome Detention Center) cerca de Miami. Primero nos dirigimos a Indiantown donde llegaron los primeros refugiados mayas, tal vez porque el sacerdote católico Frank O'Loughlin estaba protegiendo a los refugiados e inmigrantes indocumentados que llegaban a Florida. El padre inició una campaña efectiva de educación a los campesinos sobre sus derechos como seres humanos,

friend Kayuta Clouds, with whom I had worked in Guatemala on an organic agriculture project and in a school of Maya culture, science, and philosophy for the Cakchiquel Maya of Poaquil, Chimaltenango. One day in October 1980, after class Kay had gone to the market to buy his food. On his way back, as he passed in front of the Chimaltenango city park, six heavily armed men suddenly approached him, grabbed him, hit him, shoved him into a car, and took off down an unknown route. All of this took place in front of many witnesses, including national police officers, who did nothing to stop it. A few days later his body was found, brutally beaten and showing signs of torture, abandoned in the streets of Antigua.

The face of Kay's mother reflected a profound sadness. Still, she smiled when she saw me. Her greeting and her pleasure at seeing me gave me strength to continue my struggle and to denounce the injustices and the true causes of the violence, in the name of her son, who valiantly sacrificed his life for the Maya cause.

In February 1983 the Mohawk chiefs and editors of the Indian newspaper *Akwesasne Notes* unexpectedly called me and asked if I would accompany them to Florida to help the lawyers of the Florida Rural Legal Services (FRLS) and those of the American Friends Service Committee (AFSC), who were defending some Kanjobal people from San Miguel Acatán who had been detained in the Krome Detention Center of the Immigration and Naturalization Service near Miami. First we were sent to Indiantown, where the first Maya refugees came, perhaps because of the presence of the Catholic priest Frank O'Loughlin, who was protecting the refugees and undocumented immigrants arriving in Florida. This priest began an effective campaign of education in the work camps, where people's rights as human beings were being violated in many ways by the INS border patrol, the *migra*. The slogan "No firmes nada; no digas nada; llama al

frente a todo tipo de abusos de la patrulla de la frontera del INS o la "migra." El slogan "No firmes nada; no digas nada; llama al abogado" fue exitosamente puesto en práctica por los kanjobales detenidos; esto los salvó de ser deportados a Guatemala. Por otro lado los detenidos decidieron no hablar el poco español que conocían sino solamente su lengua materna kanjobal, estrategia que puso en aprietos a la "migra," quien fracasó en sus intentos de deportarlos. A eso se debía mi presencia, porque los abogados querían presentar un buen caso ante el juez de migración en favor de los kanjobales, ya que hablo el idioma, conozco la cultura, y en ese tiempo yo era uno de los poquísimos guatemaltecos que exitosamente se me había concedido asilo político. Mi experiencia y los valiosos argumentos que utilicé en mi caso ayudarían a los abogados a pelear por estos hermanos mayas. Así fue que no sólo ayudé a preparar el material y servir de intérprete, sino también me presenté como un testigo experto en la audiencia con el juez. Además se vió el apoyo de la iglesia, de los indios norteamericanos, de los "scholars," y de otras personas.

El juez fue convencido y liberó a los ocho hombres y una mujer kanjobales, profundamente conmovido por sus historias personales sufridas en Guatemala. El padre Frank se hizo responsable de estos refugiados en su parroquia en Indiantown hasta que se decidiera definitivamente el status legal de estos nueve campesinos. Este hecho dió la pauta para convertir a Indiantown en un santuario para los refugiados mayas en Florida y en general para todos los campesinos indocumentados. Mientras tanto, Rob Williams de FRLS en Immokalee y Peter Upton del AFSC de Miami continuaron asistiendo legalmente a los kanjobales con mi permanente apoyo y el del padre Frank. Ante esta situación, consulté y solicité las opiniónes y el apoyo de los Mohawks de Nueva York, el doctor Shelton Davis del Anthropology Resource Center, y los miembros del Indian Law

abogado" (Don't sign anything; don't say anything; call the lawyer) was successfully put into practice among the detained Kanjobals. This saved them from being deported to Guatemala. In addition, the detainees decided not to use the little Spanish they knew and to speak instead only their mother tongue, Kanjobal. This strategy exasperated the *migra,* who were thwarted in their attempts to deport the refugees. My presence was crucial, for the lawyers wanted to present a good case before the immigration judge in favor of the Kanjobals, and I understood the language, knew the culture, and at this time was one of the very few Guatemalans who had been successful in gaining political asylum. My experience and the successful arguments I had used in my case aided the lawyers in their fight for these Maya comrades. I not only helped to prepare the materials and served as an interpreter but also testified as an expert witness before the judge. In addition, there was support from the church, from North Americans Indians, from scholars, and from others.

The judge was convinced and released the eight Kanjobal men and one Kanjobal woman, having been profoundly moved by their personal histories of suffering in Guatemala. Father Frank took responsibility for the refugees in his parish in Indiantown until the legal status of these nine *campesinos* was finally decided. This event was the incident that converted Indiantown into a sanctuary for the Maya refugees in Florida and for undocumented people in general. Meanwhile, Rob Williams of the Florida Rural Legal Services in Immokalee and Peter Upton of the American Friends Service Committee of Miami continued to provide legal help for the Kanjobal with my assistance and that of Father Frank.

Meanwhile, I consulted with and solicited the opinions and aid of the Mohawks of New York, Dr. Shelton Davis of the Anthropology Resource Center, and members of the Indian Law

Resource Center en Washington, D.C., para la creación del Comité de Refugiados Mayas en Indiantown. A ellos les pareció buena la idea. Entonces con el apoyo local del padre Frank, nació el proyecto CORN-Maya, cuya filosofía se basa en la cultura, la identidad, y los valores indígenas de los mayas. Partiendo de este criterio, tenía el propósito de promover la defensa legal, el desarrollo económico y social, y la adaptación con dignidad de los mayas en este país.

La situación en San Miguel ya no es igual. Es difícil que la tranquilidad vuelva. El pueblo tradicional y pacífico que existía antes es sólo un sueño ahora. Los miguelenos, jacaltecos, solomeros, mames, quiches, aguacatecos, kanjobales, y otros mayas refugiados en Florida y en otros estados, como pueblo, como nación, o como grupo *no* volverán a Guatemala. Quizás algunos individuos lo harán temporalmente o definitivamente.

Prácticamente en Norteamérica hay una nueva nación indígena; es la de los Mayas en el Exilio. En vista de eso, tenemos por delante un tremendo compromiso, un arduo trabajo, una constante lucha, y una pelea continua en pro del respeto, del reconocimiento, y de la sobrevivencia.

Resource Center in Washington, D.C., in order to create a Maya refugee committee, the Comité de Refugiados Mayas, in Indiantown. They liked the idea, and with the local assistance of Father Frank O'Loughlin, the CORN-Maya project was born, basing its philosophy on the indigenous culture, identity, and values of the Maya. Evolved from these criteria, its goal is to promote legal defense, economic and social development, and the adaptation of the Maya in the United States with dignity.

The situation in San Miguel is no longer what it was. Difficult as it is to face, a return to the tranquility, to the traditional and peaceful community that existed before is now only a dream. The Migueleno, Jacalteco, Solomero, Mame, Quiche, Aguacateco, Kanjobal, and other refugee Maya in Florida and other states, as a community, as a nation, or as a group, *will not* return to Guatemala, although a few individuals may do so temporarily or permanently.

Practically speaking, there is a new Indian nation in North America—the Maya in Exile. In light of this, from now on we face a tremendous obligation, a formidable task, a constant struggle, and a continuous fight for respect, recognition, and survival.

ONE

MAYA REFUGEES AND APPLIED ANTHROPOLOGY

The Maya are the single largest group of indigenous people living in their traditional lands in North and Central America. They are not a lost or vanished people; in fact, the Maya people of Mexico, Guatemala, Belize, Honduras, and the United States number over four million. The Maya have often graced the pages of *National Geographic*, as in an October 1989 article entitled "La Ruta Maya (Garrett 1989)." The article advances an ambitious plan to save the rain forests of Mexico and Central America by transforming the Maya homelands into a vast route for the new "eco-tourism." The imaginative photograph that heralds this transformation is of a cable car suspended above the jungle from which tourists are able to view ruins, jungle, parrots, a whole scenic panorama, but without seeing people.

The Maya are still a population of magnitude and strength in Mexico and Guatemala (Early 1982). But they are also to be found walking along the rural roads of the western United States, on the streets of New York City and Los Angeles, in Oregon farm communities, and in well-to-do Florida communities like West Palm Beach. This book is concerned with those contemporary Maya who have settled in the United States, especially the four thousand or so who have adopted a small agricultural town in Florida as their new home. It is an ethnography of a people whose popular image is as members of a pre-Columbian civilization with beautiful architecture and an enigmatic culture. The Maya of this book are not the preconquest Maya, but modern Maya who have fled what Beatriz Manz (1988) has called Central America's "hidden war" in Guatemala to find a new life, often in poverty, in the United States.

Ever since the mid-nineteenth century, a myth has developed that the Maya are unconnected to their ancestors, and that the present-day people in the Maya areas of Mexico and Central America retain little of Maya culture. In trying to understand how monumental cities such as Palenque and Chichen Itza were abandoned at that time, archaeologists writing and speaking about the collapse of the "classic" Maya around the tenth century imply that the Maya people themselves somehow collapsed or disappeared. If anything, present-day Maya are described as "descendants" of the Maya, a way to describe them as devoid of classic Maya culture, history, or direct lineage. A *Newsweek* article (October 9, 1989) laments the use of pre-Columbian stones in modern Maya villages. The modern Maya are portrayed in this and other popular articles as people who have turned into modern peasants with little knowledge of their own history. "Yucatan archaeologists," the article explains, "long worried about the damage wreaked by acid rain and artifact smugglers, have recently detected a more prevalent and potentially more dangerous menace: the modern Mayas" (Padgett 1989:83).

Guatemalan Maya refugees are part of a striking sequence of involuntary migrations that has affected Central America in the past ten years. An estimated two million refugees have fled the conflicts throughout Central America (Manz 1988:7); nearly a quarter of a million of these are from Guatemala. As Roger Zetter notes, "alienation, persecution and forced migration are among the most profoundly disturbing human experiences" (Zetter 1988:1). This is true for the Maya, who have not only been forced from their villages but have now crossed the cultural, geographic, and national borders of Guatemala and Mexico to come to the United States. While the more visible confrontations in Nicaragua and El Salvador attract much more media attention, Guatemala continues to produce a major flow of refugees (Doughty 1988; Ferris 1987).

In contrast to other refugee cases in the world, Central American refugees from Guatemala call into question traditional and legal ways of understanding forced migration. The United Nations definition limits asylum to the first country encountered. Refugees from Guatemala did not migrate *to* another country of "first asylum" so much as they fled *from* a country of devastating violence. Many Maya refugees from the highlands went to Mexico to seek asylum in the first country they encountered. But there they were harassed by Guatemalan government troops, who raided refugee camps in Chiapas in the early 1980s. These raids showed that "first asylum" could not be found in Mexico (Valencia 1984). For many, real asylum means the more perilous life of undocumented aliens in the United States.

The Guatemalan government changed leadership in the mid- and late 1980s. One sign of the change was the 1985 election of Vinicio Cerezo as a civilian president from the Christian Democrat party, which replaced the military leadership responsible for programs of village destruction. With the election of a second civilian president in 1990, the hold of the military on the government has further weakened. Because of this shift from a military to a civilian government, many people believe that the lives of Guatemalan refugees are now safe. But returning refugees have not been able to resume their lives. Those who chance a return to Guatemala do not fare well. There they are picked up by the military or migrate to Guatemala City to live a miserable existence in the informal economic sector. Their lands have been confiscated, and they find extreme restrictions on personal freedoms, forced concentration of people in "model" villages, and great resentment from villagers who stayed behind (Manz 1988). Killings and disappearances continue into the 1990s, so that Guatemala is still considered a serious violator of human rights by international groups such as Amnesty International.

The Kanjobal and other Guatemalan Maya who have come to Florida are a different kind of refugees from those normally encountered. They are cultural refugees who have migrated in large family and community groups. Boothby (1986) and others have pointed out that political violence in Central America involves children in much greater numbers than in other areas. Children are the combatants. Regular army and insurgency troops conscript children who are old enough to manage weapons (Ressler, Boothby, and Steibock 1988). Children are also victims of a high proportion of the violence in the region, especially in Guatemala. A fourteen-year-old Guatemalan Maya boy described his experience to psychologist Neil Boothby as we sat in a Florida living room one afternoon:

> PEDRO MARTINEZ: They would come and they would ask, "Where are the men or the boys?" Then they would take them.
>
> NEIL BOOTHBY: What would they do to them?
>
> PEDRO MARTINEZ: They would take them or threaten them or kill them. They killed hundreds.
>
> NEIL BOOTHBY: They killed hundreds. And why do you think they did this?
>
> PEDRO MARTINEZ: Because they thought we were the guerrillas or we were helping the guerrillas. They would say,

"Where are all the guerrillas?" or "You are the guerrillas"
and then they would take them.
NEIL BOOTHBY: And what would they do to them?
PEDRO MARTINEZ: They would take them and they would
kill them, I think. They would take them.

Throughout the 1980s, everyday events witnessed by children resulted in the wholesale migration of families and entire
communities away from areas of violence and terror. Guatemalan army figures list some four hundred villages that were
destroyed in the early part of the decade (Boothby 1986:28).

The U.S. position toward Guatemala has been a complex
arrangement of interference and ignorance. The U.S. government has supported Guatemala since helping to overthrow the
Arbenz government there in the 1950s (Fried 1983). Guatemala
became a tourist mecca in the 1960s, was singled out by President Carter as one of the worst human rights violators in
the 1970s, and was championed in the 1980s as a showcase
for a transition from military to civilian rule (Helton 1989).
Throughout the period of the worst violence in Guatemala,
from 1979 through 1986, the United States supplied Guatemala
with military supplies such as helicopters and trucks. A Supreme Court ruling in 1990 reopened the political asylum cases
that had been denied over the past ten years. This ruling, known
as the "ABC" ruling after the American Baptist Churches,
which brought the suit to the court, provided a ray of hope for
the thousands of Guatemalans who had been denied asylum
since 1980.

One problem facing the Kanjobal and other Maya who immigrated to Florida is the lack of knowledge in the United States
about the conflicts of Guatemala. There is little interest in
discussing the complex political setting of Guatemala in gen-

eral. News reports are few, and the media tend to cover other Central American countries in greater depth.

The Kanjobal and neighboring Maya now find themselves in a problematic situation that shows little hope of resolution. They are living in exile, a group of people who have been forced into a diaspora stretching from southern Mexico to Canada. It is difficult for those of us whose families have lived in the New World only a few generations to appreciate the Maya attachment to their lands and homes (Bizairo Uzpán 1985). The Maya continue to live on lands their ancestors inhabited three thousand years ago. Even with their lands, social organization, and culture under assault by the Mexican and Central American forces of discrimination, they continue to preserve as much of their land and culture as is feasible. Today in Guatemala there are associations of Maya professionals, such as lawyers and teachers, who fund traditional keepers of the faith. Barbara Tedlock recognized the beginnings of these new associations during her fieldwork in Momostenango in the late 1970s: "A group of them [wealthier merchants and weavers], nearly all elders, recently founded a religious organization that stands outside both Catholic Action and the traditional confraternities, while at the same time reaffirming the importance of saints and of Momostecan cultural identity: It is a brotherhood (*hermanidad*), modeled after the ladino brotherhoods of Momostenango" (Tedlock 1982:42). Since that time, such organizations have sprung up in many communities, and the conservation of traditional knowledge is consciously being cultivated. These traditionalists are considered treasures by their communities, because it is they who continue to use the ancient calendar, carry out rituals, and maintain cultural resistance in the face of the violence that has swept their lands. The groups have been seen by some scholars as part of a conservative Indian bourgeoisie whose "intentions were directed at formulating a worldview that did not question their position as a class" (Arias 1990:238). I disagree with such class-based analyses. During the 1980s, when the violence in Guatemala became directed at ethnic groups and not just at social classes, many of these people were killed or fled from Guatemala along with their poorer neighbors.

One of these traditionalists, Luis Francisco, who is also a musician, stayed at my home in Florida for a while. As part of my own work with the Maya in Florida, I had organized a concert of Maya marimba music for the Florida Museum of Natural History. Luis was in South Florida when the marimba group was assembled for the concert, so he came with them. One day, as he stood outside in our front yard, Luis began naming in Jacaltec Maya the birds that he heard singing in the trees. "How did you learn so much about the birds?" I asked. "My father is a diviner," he said. "I guess I always liked to pay attention to birds and things like that." I asked what he was doing in Florida. He had not suffered persecution as so many other people I had met, and he did not have any expressed interest in either the government or the guerrilla position in Guatemala. He just said, "There are people here who we can't forget. They have to be reminded of the days and the ways to do Maya prayers, rituals, wedding ceremonies, and so forth." He talked about memorizing the day names of the Maya calendar and the importance of each (Tedlock 1982). He told how bless-ings of agricultural land have to include references to people several generations past as well as several generations into the future.

In late 1982 a few Kanjobal Maya people from Guatemala arrived in the agricultural town of Indiantown, Florida. They had been brought there by a Mexican crew leader because of the abundant work in the citrus groves, vegetable farms, and ranches of south-central Florida. Like many migrants, these first few immigrants told their family and friends about the abundance of work and the haven they had found in Florida. Although Florida was thousands of miles away from the mountainous region of Guatemala that these families called home, it was a recognizable environment. Work in Florida was, for them, like work "on the coast" of Guatemala; the weather was hot and humid, the work contractual and at times plentiful, and the housing conditions bearable though not adequate.

Like traditional Maya migrants to the coast of Guatemala from the indigenous communities of the mountains (Lovell 1988), the people who came to Indiantown thought that they would stay no more than a few months. Indiantown was just one more small community in a string of small towns stretching from the Guatemalan border up through Canada. The idea that these small communities were parts of different nations was hardly considered by many of the first refugees. Arturo Xunek, a man in his late fifties, talked to me about the state of Florida and the community of Indiantown as being part of Mexico. The state of Chiapas, Mexico, borders on the traditional homeland of the Kanjobal Maya. To Arturo Xunek, everything that was not his home was either Guatemalan land or Mexican land. But while Arturo's sense of geographic boundaries was blurred, his sense of history and society was not. He had spent two years making his way across Mexico to find a place to live in Indiantown and was quick to point out the evolving conflict between the Guatemalans and other Hispanics in the town.

The Kanjobal Maya make up one of more than twenty six distinct Maya language and culture groups of Guatemala. Because of the traditional isolation of people like the Kanjobal (Davis 1970), the first language in their homelands was always Maya, with Spanish a distant second. While some of the languages, such as Kanjobal and Jacaltec Maya, are mutually understandable, most are quite different from one another (Kaufman

1974). Differences in pronunciation, vocabulary, and grammar are as prevalent as the differences between European languages such as French and Spanish.

The Kanjobal homeland lies in the Cuchumatan Mountains of northwestern Guatemala, in the province of Huehuetenango. The Mexican anthropologist Gonzalo Aguirre Beltran (1967) referred to these mountainous regions in Mexico and Central America as "regions of refuge." They were places where indigenous cultures could be maintained because the lands were inaccessible and little valued. According to MacLeod (1973), economic exploitation of the resources of Guatemala by Spaniards in the colonial period led to a decimation of the indigenous land and population, forcing the most conservative and indomitable groups to seek refuge in the highlands (Wolf 1982). As Lovell (1988) points out, over the past fifty years, the Kanjobal and other Maya were pushed higher and higher into altitudes where subsistence agriculture had to be supplemented through migratory labor.

The traditional Maya agricultural system of *milpa* is a shifting cultivation program in which corn is carefully grown in fields along with other crops. The other crops include those important for subsistence (such as beans and squash) as well as those used for other purposes, including for sale (such as coffee, fruits, and citrus). The extreme altitudes of many of the Kanjobal lands are not suitable for much more than subsistence farming, so a tradition of wage labor migration to the Pacific coast of Guatemala developed.

The Kanjobal Maya of Guatemala live in dispersed settlements, or *aldeas*. Many who migrated to the United States came from the area surrounding the municipal center of San Miguel Acatán. Most of these *aldeas* contain one or two extended families of up to twenty people. Their subsistence land base had become less and less able to sustain them, as Shelton

Davis points out in his study of land tenure in the area (1970). In San Miguel, shops, markets, and services added to the economy of the Kanjobal. Because land in the highlands was scarce and agriculture poor, the Kanjobal were interested in innovative ways of improving their economy. Interest in agricultural cooperatives, new crops, and education was high before extensive violence swept the area in the early 1980s (Davis and Hodson 1982). Arturo Arias (1990) shows how the events described by Camposeco in the Introduction, such as the literacy programs, the miners' strike, and the rise of indigenous insurgency, developed into a new kind of articulation between the Maya and the Guatemalan state in the 1970s.

The political and social life of Maya villages such as those around San Miguel has been examined by anthropologists and linguists (Martin 1977). Oliver La Farge wrote one of the classic studies of the Maya based on his travels in and around Jacaltenango in the 1920s. His two books on the area, *Santa Eulalia* (1947) and (with Douglas Byers) *The Year Bearer's People* (1931), describe the culture of the Jacaltec and Kanjobal people as rich in intellectual tradition. The title *The Year Bearer's People* is a recognition of the heritage of calendrical knowledge that he found. Studies of other Maya communities in Guatemala such as those by La Farge (1940), Wagley (1949), Bunzel (1952), Reina (1974), Carmack (1981), and Annis (1987) have all pointed out the internal strength of local political and social structures. Along with the national institutions of modern Guatemala, Maya communities in the highlands developed a successful set of institutions ranging from the extensive moral authority of the lineage diviners (Tedlock 1982) to the civil-religious hierarchies (Camara 1952; Cancian 1965). Nash's *Machine Age Maya* (1967) is an especially insightful look at how traditional Maya agriculture can coexist with factory work in a community.

All of these studies stress the importance of clan and lineage kinship structures rooted in centuries-long attachment to particular communities. Tedlock notes that each lineage and clan in Momostenango is the basic social unit and that, at the time of her fieldwork, over three hundred priest-shamans formed a corporate group linking the lineages together (Tedlock 1982:35).

The growing violence of the late 1970s and 1980s in Guatemala placed such traditional features of Maya *aldeas* and villages under siege:

> JERONIMO CAMPOSECO: They have their traditional, how can I say it, Maya priest, and he knows Maya calendars, the sacred days. He is a spiritual advisor for the people. And he has helpers, you know, and he does those ceremonies. But, in 1981, the soldiers killed practically the last spiritual leader of the people.
> ALLAN BURNS: Why would they kill the spiritual leaders?
> JERONIMO CAMPOSECO: The excuse of the soldiers was that he was making ritual ceremonies in favor of the guerrilla. So what he was doing was praying. He was making beads in order to have peace, because the Kanjobal people are a very peaceful people. They are Mayas, you know. The Mayas are peaceful people.

The complete destruction of Maya communities released an outpouring of concern by many anthropologists. Davis and Hodson's *Witness to Political Violence in Guatemala* (1982) and Carmack's *Harvest of Violence* (1988), as well as reports by *Cultural Survival Quarterly* (Falla 1983, Burns 1988), Painter (1987), the Washington Office on Latin America (1988), the Asociación para el Avance de las Ciencias Sociales (1990), and Frelick (1991), register the disgust scholars felt at the news of the violence that swept Guatemala.

For the people who lived through these attacks, one survival strategy was to flee to the north. Unlike many migrants from

Central America, the Maya who have come to Florida since 1982 first arrived as families. Children with one or more parents, uncles, cousins, brothers-in-law, and sisters-in-law all traveled together. They came in vans, paying several thousand dollars for a trip from Arizona or California to Florida. When the violence that drove them from Guatemala was still raging in the mid-1980s, advocates in the United States often drove them from city to city until they arrived in West Palm Beach, Immokalee, or Indiantown, where work and other people like them could be found. After the first five years passed, however, family group immigration was replaced by the immigration of young men. These were often individuals whose families had earlier fled their hamlets and tried to survive in Guatemala City or Mexico. Now, as teenagers, young men from these families have begun to arrive in the United States in search of work and identity.

While the Maya who arrived in the United States came from many different communities, most of those who came to Florida came from the area around San Miguel Acatán in Huehuetenango, Guatemala. Much of what is written in the following chapters centers on the majority of U.S. Maya who come from San Miguel. Here in the United States, they are generally referred to as the "Kanjobal Maya," although their language is spelled "Q'anjob'al" in Guatemala. By the early 1990s, however, the Kanjobal Maya were joined by more and more people from other Maya communities in Guatemala as well as many people who identified themselves as "ladinos" or non-Maya. Now, in places like Indiantown, as Jerónimo Camposeco points out in the Introduction, it is as common to hear the Maya languages of Jacaltec, Quiche, or Cakchiquel as it is to hear Guatemalan Spanish.

There have been traditional Maya in Yucatan, Guatemala, and other parts of Central America throughout the past five hundred years of European colonization. It would be a mistake, however, to look at these people as if they were only modern representatives of ancient Maya culture. The Maya today are modern and alert to the changing world around them. They have changed and evolved as quickly as any other society in the past five hundred years since the European world encountered them. Today Maya people are sophisticated citizens who are adapting to the transformations of the world like anybody else. For some that has meant escaping from the brutality of their own government and migrating to the United States. For others it has meant adapting to new countries and seeking ways to preserve their heritage. That adaption has included making contact with people in the United States and collaborating with them for legal assistance, social welfare, and scholarship. Some, like Victor Montejo, have published books in English about the terrorism in Guatemala (Montejo 1987) as well as about traditional myths and stories (Montejo 1991). Many of the Maya of Indiantown, Florida, have collaborated with anthropologists both in Guatemala and in the United States. The result has been the development of an anthropology with a decided applied orientation among the Maya, especially here in the United States.

Applied anthropologists are often much more likely than other social scientists to work firsthand with people as advocates as well as researchers (Adams 1953). As Erve Chambers (1987) notes, applied anthropology today is concerned with issues such as health, education, international development, and social impacts of government-sponsored change programs. An older conception of the approach by George Foster was broader: "When anthropologists utilize their theoretical concepts, factual knowledge, and research methodologies in programs meant to ameliorate contemporary social, economic, and technological problems, they are engaging in applied anthropology" (Foster 1969:vii).

One intellectual inspiration for our work in Indiantown was

the applied community work of the Cornell-Peru Project in the 1950s and 1960s (Holmberg et al. 1962; Holmberg et al. 1965; Dobyns, Doughty, and Lasswell 1971; Nuñez del Prado 1973; Lynch 1981; Doughty 1987). The Cornell-Peru Project, known as the "Vicos project," endeavored to bring about the empowerment of people living on a Peruvian *hacienda*. The project leased the *hacienda* from the landowners, and set about developing mechanisms whereby the local residents could improve agriculture, schooling, the local political structure, and health. The project has been criticized on many grounds, including showing a lack of concern for the role of women, becoming directly involved in social change in a foreign country, and failing to sustain the changes over a long period of time. Some of the criticisms are warranted, but many simply represent disapproval of taking an applied approach at all.

One of the most impressive features of the Vicos project was the number of people involved in the research. Like the famous community studies done in the United States during the 1930s and 1940s, such as *Yankee City* (Warner 1956), the project involved numerous fieldworkers who carried out many different tasks and subprojects. The work in Indiantown has been similar in this regard. As part of the articulation between the University of Florida and the community, Indiantown has hosted a number of anthropologists. Students have worked on issues of women's health, urban planning, Haitian adaptation, labor and employment, education, history, and child health, in the community and surrounding environs. Other anthropologists, such as Sandy Davis of the World Bank, Duncan Earl of Vanderbilt University, Brian Page of the University of Miami, and Laura Martin of Cleveland State University, have visited the community. The Introduction to this study attests to the important role of indigenous anthropologist and Maya refugee Jerónimo Camposeco. A concentrated effort was made to include as many

anthropologists as fieldworkers in the community in order provide as much assistance as possible and to open up opportunities both for the people of the community and for other
anthropologists.

Unlike the Vicos project, however, the thrust of applied anthropology with the Maya of Florida has not centered on an
overall master plan. Instead, the projects that have been completed are based on an ongoing dialogue between representatives of the community; social service agencies involved with
the educational, health, and social well-being of the community; and individual anthropologists from the University of
Florida.

One of the responsibilities that comes with the satisfaction
of working in a profession such as anthropology is making
knowledge useful for people. Lewis Henry Morgan, an anthropologist who worked in the mid-nineteenth century with
the Iroquois, helped with land claims suits that the Iroquois
brought against the U.S. government in the 1870s. Margaret
Mead had a long and fruitful career working in education as
well as anthropology. Anthropologists today, as Elizabeth Eddy
points out in *Applied Anthropology in the Americas* (Eddy and
Partridge 1986), have found roles as urban planners, business
executives, and legal advocates. When I first began working
with the Maya, I wondered whether any skills I had could be
useful. I spoke one of the Maya languages in addition to Spanish
and English. I had authored books, reports, and articles. I had
worked with media and knew students who were looking for
master's and Ph.D. research. All of these abilities have been
useful. Over the years since 1982, my own role has been varied
within the growing Maya community of Florida. I have co-
produced, with a professional filmmaker, several documentaries on the Maya in an effort to educate more people about their
plight. Research projects with funding from the Labor Depart-

ment and other sources have been developed. Student internships focusing on the Maya and other groups in the community, such as Haitians, have generated a book (Miralles 1988) and many articles and master's theses. I have served as a board member on an indigenous association and helped it achieve legal, nonprofit status.

I have lived, traveled, and worked with the Maya as a normal part of my life, while I continued to teach and do other research at the University of Florida (Burns 1989b). The Maya of Florida are not a group of people that I visit when I "do fieldwork" in a distant land; they are friends and fellow Floridians who call me at my office or at home, who have joined with my family in baptisms and marriages, who ask for favors for their children, and who visit when they are in town. Maya professionals, such as Jerónimo Camposeco, travel with me to anthropology conventions where we give joint papers (Burns and Camposeco 1991).

Applied anthropology is a strategy that is both theoretical and practical. On a theoretical level, this applied work is concerned with the extent to which immigration to the United States is a result of either "push" or "pull" factors. To what extent have the Kanjobal Maya of Florida been pulled here by the lure of steady work, safety, and the community structure of a small town? It is impossible to maintain that these social and economic forces are not important in the decisions of people to migrate in general, and in the decisions of the Maya to come to Florida in particular. Even in the community of Indiantown, some local residents regard the efforts of the Catholic church and the Maya organizations that have arisen as contributing to the pull of people from Central America to this small U.S. town.

What is very apparent when talking with the Maya is that they were "pushed" in very brutal ways from their homelands as

well. Stories of atrocities, destruction, and chaos abound when
the Maya talk about living in Guatemala in the 1980s. A conversation with one priest who works with immigrants in Florida
was revealing:

> ALLAN BURNS: What has it been like to work with the Kan-
> jobal? How are they different from other groups that have
> come here?
>
> FRANK O'LOUGHLIN: We've had evidences of the real cul-
> tural shock, and we've had evidences of the difficulty of
> adapting to this real cash culture. First of all, I don't know
> how people make it. To travel through Mexico, right, is the
> most incredible trick. And to do it in a foreign language—
> Spanish was a foreign language for them. And all the un-
> knowns of the journey. I talked to one family who got on a
> train in Mexico and made a long journey by train and I
> asked them why they got on the train and they said, "Large
> groups of people were getting on the train, and it had to be
> a good thing to do." They had no sense of any goal towards
> which they were headed. They were literally just respond-
> ing to the terror behind them. And they had only one goal
> and that was to distance themselves as far as possible from
> this terror. And I couldn't imagine that. That defined "refu-
> gee" for me all over again. People with absolutely no goal,
> no place to go, but just simply something to be running
> from.

A second theoretical issue raised by this study is that of
identity. Ethnicity is an identity that makes sense in contrast to
the presence of other ethnic groups in a society. Guatemala is
fairly limited in this regard. Besides the Maya, the only other
ethnic group of any size are the ladinos, or non-Maya. The Maya
are not a unified group in Guatemala or for that matter in any of
the areas where they presently reside. There are over thirty-

three recognized Maya languages, many as different from one another as the European languages. Even the violence of the 1980s in Guatemala was not uniform. Some areas, such as the Cuchumatan Mountains, were hit hard by both guerrilla and military actions, while others a few hundred kilometers away were untouched.

Still, in Guatemala, the Maya were the only indigenous group, and no other groups vied for identity with them. In contrast, in the United States, the Maya find themselves one of many minorities, even in small towns. They are aware of Cambodians, Haitians, Mexicans, other Central Americans, African Americans, and Native Americans, to name a few. Their cultural identity is now defined in relation to these other groups. The sense they have of being "Maya" is now redefined in an ethnically pluralistic society.

Ethnicity is more than an internal feature of an individual's or group's personality. Ethnicity is also something that is imposed from without, a label that outsiders apply to a group of people (De Vos and Romanucci-Ross 1982). In the case of the Guatemalan Maya, their identity is shifting from one of culture to one of work. The Maya here in the United States become identified with their jobs, so that they are now "migrant workers," not indigenous Maya. Failing this, they are identified with their legal status, and become "illegals," part of that undifferentiated mass of immigrants who have no official status with the U.S. Immigration and Naturalization Service. This external sense of identity blends with the internal one for each person (Burns 1989a). Consequently, the Maya of Florida who have been in the United States for four, five, or six years are quite different from the Maya of Mexico or Guatemala.

A third theoretical issue addressed in this book is the nature of anthropological representation. For many anthropologists, the proper form of ethnographic reporting is a traditional social science monograph. Under this approach, anthropology is guided by careful observations, attention to patterns that are observable and documented, and a search for causes and relationships. Reporting takes the form of a narrative in which summaries of data, a few direct quotations, and conclusions related to theoretical perspectives are expected. Pertti J. and Gretel H. Pelto (1976) describe this approach well in their book *Anthropological Research.* Less sophisticated, but still very useful as examples of this approach, are James Spradley's *The Ethnographic Interview* (1979) and *Participant Observation* (1980). Most recently, H. Russell Bernard's *Methods in Anthropology* (1988) has provided a clear statement of this approach.

Complementary to this is a second approach to reporting, one that is dialogic and interpretive. As I have argued elsewhere in regard to linguistic materials (Burns 1980, 1992, and forthcoming), a dialogic approach takes a great interest in the texts that are collected in the course of interviewing or doing research. The approach is more conscious of the role of the ethnographer in the enterprise and even of the writing style used to communicate ethnographic information. Books such as Marcus and Fischer's *Anthropology as Cultural Critique* (1986) have discussed this mix of self-conscious reporting, interpretation of text, and an interest in history as well as an ethnographic moment in time. During an earlier period of anthropology, the angry and yet shrewd work of Jules Henry in *Culture Against Man* (1963), which admirably combines passion and applied interpretation, showed how national ideology and everyday family behavior could be interpreted in innovative ways. A more restrained example of an interpretive and dialogic method is found in the collection of articles by Dennis Tedlock, *The Spoken Word and the Work of Interpretation* (1983).

This book combines a traditional social science approach with a dialogic, interpretive style. Much of what follows is based on descriptions and analyses that are well within a social science framework. I once asked Harry Wolcott whether his work could be considered a kind of "educational anthropology research." He replied that the label did not matter; what was important was whether or not it was good research. In the same sense, the aim of this work is to provide an account of the Maya as they have appeared in the United States over the past ten years. Whether or not the account is "interpretive" or "positivistic social science" is not as important as the research. The pleasure of doing anthropology and writing a book like this comes from the opportunity to combine both.

I have quoted as many voices as possible to communicate the experience of the Maya in Florida. There are the voices of the Maya themselves, the voices of their detractors speaking through newspaper articles and epitaphs, and the voices of the "helping community" that has evolved in places such as Indiantown.

This book reflects the different relationships I have had with Maya people in Florida. The themes of the book reflect a mix of applied research and advocacy. A high value has been placed on the way the Maya themselves have described their lives and their adaptation to the United States. The chapters are presented in a way that attempts to convey both personal interpretations of what it means to be struggling for Maya cultural survival in a foreign land and a more general understanding of how people in a small community react to the influx of several thousand people from another country and another society.

Chapter Two, "Escape and Arrival," describes the political and social background of the Guatemalan Maya immigrants in the United States. Personal accounts of several immigrants are used to show the strategies for leaving Guatemala and journeying to the United States. The chapter continues with excerpts from interviews with Jerónomo Camposeco, and in this way puts his Introduction to this book in the context of the narratives of other immigrants.

Chapter Three, "Life Crisis and Ritual," introduces the Maya of Florida through a baptism held in Indiantown. The participation of people in the baptismal ceremony and in the accompanying party illustrates the forces that confront the Maya, how they interact with the institutions of the community, and how they have organized themselves through traditional and new organizations to make their voice heard in the United States.

Chapter Four, "The Maya in Community and Ethnic Context," looks at the farmworker community in South Florida where the greatest number of Maya live. The chapter begins with a discussion of Indiantown as a small town with a history of migrant labor immigration. The influx of Maya into the labor and social context of the town is discussed, using a formal survey of the Maya, Mexicans, and Haitians in the community. The chapter examines this new role of the Maya as one of several ethnic groups in small farmworker towns in the United States.

Chapter Five, "Work and Changes in Social Structure," continues the community study approach begun in the fourth chapter by exploring how wage labor in agriculture and other low-wage jobs has influenced Maya social structure in the United States. The chapter also examines how U.S. immigration policy, especially the 1986 Immigration Reform and Control Act, affects the Maya immigrants.

Chapter Six, "Conflict and the Evolution of a New Maya Identity," describes how identity for the Maya has changed both among the Maya and outside the Maya community. The process of identity shift through adaptation to the institutions of the United States is described, as is the change in image of the Maya from victims of oppression to poor farmworkers.

Chapter Seven, "Visual Anthropology and the Maya," explores how applied projects in the community have been developed. The primary example used in the chapter is a collaborative set of video documentaries made with Maya associates on topics such as refugee status, a community celebration, and women's health care.

Chapter Eight, "Always Maya," examines the lives of several young Maya people who now face new problems of life in the United States. The chapter discusses strategic adaptation among Maya immigrants to the United States and their continuing struggle for their own community.

TWO

ESCAPE AND ARRIVAL

The number of Maya people who have come to the United States as refugees is difficult to assess. Since 1981 the number of Guatemalan refugees inside and outside Guatemala has been estimated as being as high as 600,000, with up to 200,000 in the United States (Zolberg, Suhrke, and Aguayo 1989:212). Of these, only a very few have been given political asylum. Between 1983 and 1986, when the first wave of close to 100,000 Guatemalans fled to the United States, only 14 petitions for political asylum were granted while 1,461 were denied (United States President's Advisory Committee for Refugees 1986:9). The numbers of people applying for either temporary or permanent worker status, those receiving legal papers through one of the provisions of the Immigration and Reform Control Act of 1986, and those here illegally have not been assessed.

Nor are there accurate figures for the number of Mayas in Florida. According to one newspaper account in late 1988, there were probably between fifteen and twenty thousand Maya in the state at that time (Palm Beach *Post*, Dec. 12, 1988). Of this number, probably close to five thousand live in Indiantown during the harvest season. Other communities with significant Maya populations include West Palm Beach, Homestead, Boynton Beach, Immokalee, and Okeechobee. These communities each have between five hundred and several thousand Maya immigrants. Small groups composed of individuals and families are found in most other agricultural communities in the state. But Indiantown is the historic, cultural, and numeric center of the Maya in the state. Indiantown and Los Angeles are considered the two major centers of Maya immigration in the United States.

As we saw in Chapter One, the violence in Guatemala in the 1980s was overwhelming for many Maya groups. Hundreds of villages were destroyed, lands were appropriated, and people were tortured and murdered with a ferocity that traumatized much of the indigenous population. The Maya of northwestern Guatemala were caught between the military forces of the government and the guerrilla movement. The guerrilla movement sought food, recruits, and ideological legitimacy from the Maya. The military sought to destroy the subsistence base of the guerrilla movement by a scorched-earth policy of rural destruction.

Not all Maya were caught by the military violence, nor were all communities in Guatemala affected. Some groups were able simply to stay isolated and outside of the zones of conflict. Others sided with the government in order to save their villages. Still others stood up to both the government forces and the guerrillas and were left alone. But many were not so fortunate. The area of the Cuchumatan Mountains was especially susceptible to both guerrilla and military campaigns through the 1980s. This chapter focuses on the stories of some of the people from this region who have now come to the United States.

The Maya who fled this modern devastation of their culture, their homes, and their families did not know where they were going or what they would find. Once in Mexico they set up temporary camps, which were soon raided by the Guatemalan military (Carmack 1988). Forty-two thousand of them were given refugee status by the Mexican government and put in camps near the Guatemalan border. When the Guatemalan army made several attacks on the camps in 1982 and 1983, several thousand were taken to isolated lands in the states of Campeche and Quintana Roo, Mexico.

One community leader, Joaquim Can, recounted the forced journey between the camps in Chiapas and Campeche:

> ALLAN BURNS: What was it like to travel from the camps in Chiapas to Campeche?
> JOAQUIM CAN: They brought us in big school buses from Chiapas. It took several weeks to bring us all here. I remember that at night they would put us in big warehouses and we had to all sleep on the floor next to each other. It was crowded and many people died, especially children and those who had infections. There was no sanitation and no way to care for those of us who were sick. Many people died.

In Campeche, the refugees constructed stick shacks with corrugated cardboard roofs. In 1989, when I interviewed residents of the camps, the same cardboard was there, only now the rains and storms had opened many houses to the elements. Despite the pathetic conditions, however, people preferred to live here than to live near the border or return to Guatemala.

Those who could fled farther north, through Mexico and into the United States. They crossed deserts at night, where they saw the bodies of people who had gotten lost in the wilderness of the border, and eventually they arrived in Phoenix and other cities. Once in the United States many applied for political asylum, while the majority entered the illegal alien world.

Receiving political asylum has been an important hope for many of the Maya. During the early years of the Maya immigration to the United States and especially to Florida, American

Friends Service Committee and Florida Rural Legal Services worked to secure documentation for political asylum cases. As more and more Maya arrived in the United States, however, asylum hearings turned hopeless; only a small handful of applicants achieved legal status through these means. Application for political asylum was still a viable strategy in the short term, however, since it enabled those Maya who applied for the status to receive temporary work permits. This temporary status allowed people to work legally and have access to hospitals and other facilities.

One of the problems with applying for political asylum status for the Maya was the fear that had been engendered in Guatemala and in the United States concerning government institutions. Refugees feared that providing their names or any information about their families to a lawyer or an immigration judge would lead to their immediate deportation to Guatemala. For this reason, individuals were loath to step into the limelight of a court hearing, especially when it became well known that asylum application hearings seemed always to lead to denial.

The case of one woman, Maria Gonzalez, is illustrative of the summary nature of the hearings. Paralegals wrote up their experience with the case in a letter to the public after her immigration hearing:

> From the first defendant, Juan Francisco, the judge heard of the brutal massacre of eleven men, including his father and two brothers, in his village of Ixcanac. Juan was away working on a coffee plantation during the massacre and received a warning from his mother never to return. Another defendant, Carlos Juan, spoke of the killings in the town of San Rafael by guerrillas of the people who did not support their movement. Maria Ana, the last defendant to be heard, described in detail how she witnessed the army massacre of

El Mul in which eleven men were killed, and on the stand
Maria described to the court how many soldiers stormed
into her home and brutally beat and hacked her father and
two brothers to death with machetes. The soldiers also beat
women and children, stole the villagers' animals, possessions, and burned homes to the ground.

The contention of the authorities all along has been that
the Kanjobal people have come here for economic reasons
rather than fleeing political violence. Another position of
the government is that the refugees should have gone to
UN-sponsored refugee camps in Mexico rather than continue on to the United States. Judge Foster told the defense
attorneys that it was not enough that one's family had been
killed for one to prove persecution and qualify for asylum.

In many ways the trials showed the cultural conflicts between a Maya people . . . and the court. An example was
Maria. Confident in the telling of the brutality she experienced, she nonetheless is not even sure of the months of
the year, is unschooled in numbers and mathematics, and
during her long flight she was often sick and unable to document how long she remained in each place. So afraid was
she by what she had witnessed that she assumed a false
name in Guatemala to protect herself, and continued using
it when caught by the immigration authorities and put in
detention in the United States. (Camposeco, Silvestre, and
Davey 1986)

It is difficult to convince the U.S. immigration authorities of
the reality of the violence and fear that are at the heart of the
Maya immigration to the United States, and attitudes about
work and being a productive member of society contribute to
misunderstanding as well. Maya people take great pride in their
dedication and commitment to work. Their abilities to work

well in diverse places such as the mountains of Guatemala, coastal coffee plantations, and now the migrant streams of the United States are a source of pride. To work hard and long is a value assumed to be appreciated in any country. When Maya women or men are asked why they are here in the United States, it is much more common for them to say that they came to work than to say that they came to escape repression. The violence, the betrayal of families and communities by neighbors, and the brutality of the Guatemalan government during the 1980s are issues that are simultaneously overwhelming and difficult to express. It is much easier to tell someone that you came to the United States because you are a good worker, in the hope that this virtue will be better received than will a sad story of your homeland. A newspaper article titled "Strangers in a Strange Land" (Palm Beach *Post*, Aug. 19, 1990) quoted a Maya who was learning English. The first phrase he proudly spoke was, "I need a good work."

The irony of this is that identifying oneself as a good worker, or in immigration terms, an "economic refugee," is the one sure way not to have a chance at gaining legal status through political asylum. Economic refugees are popularly seen as workers who take jobs from U.S. citizens, even though this is not so, and as unskilled laborers, even though many of the Maya once held positions as shopkeepers, cooperative officials, and schoolteachers. Economic refugees are seen as a drain on the U.S. economy because of the remittances they send back home. As George Waldroup, the assistant district director of the INS in Miami, said in a newspaper interview, "Most of these claims are based on economic need, but there is no such thing as economic asylum" (Palm Beach *Post*, Aug. 22, 1990).

A final problem with political asylum as a strategy for achieving legal status in the United States is the time that it takes for Maya people to travel from Guatemala to the United

States. The United States is not a country of "first asylum" for most of the Maya. A very few have managed to fly directly to the United States, but the vast majority who come by land often spend months or even years moving surreptitiously through Mexico. Sometimes individuals spend a year or more in Mexico earning enough money to move slowly toward the U.S. border. Once here, they continue with the same strategies of being unobtrusive migrant workers.

José Xunche, a recent arrival to Florida, had spent several years in Mexico, working in the oil fields of Tabasco and in a restaurant in Mexico City, before coming to the United States:

ALLAN BURNS: When was the last time you were in Guatemala?

JOSE XUNCHE: I left on January 10, 1982, and went to Mexico for two years. I heard that the military was going to come into our hamlet. I came back in 1984. I lived near Rio Azul and every day the army would come there with a truck of guerrilla captives. They would stand at the bridge, cut them up with machetes, and throw them into the river. Half of them weren't dead but they just threw them in with the dead ones. I couldn't stay, so I left and made my way up here.

Rodrigo Antonio, another immigrant, talked with Julian Arturo, a University of Florida anthropology student from Colombia, about his journey from Guatemala through Mexico:

Well, it was for the war. There in Guatemala. In my town. I am from San Miguel. But I am from Guatemala. Well, then, when there was war there it was hard for us to leave. Also we didn't have any money. Then finally I left there, fleeing. I left without hardly saying goodbye to my family because of the fear I had of the army, the ones that were killing people. It was of the government, as we say. The guerrilla was also active, killing people once in a while. But it was the army that I feared more; I feared that they would come and kill me. For example, if you went out to work there and the army came upon you, it was really easy for them to kill you, because the army could do it there. The guerrilla was up in the mountains, but the army could come upon you on the road or in the *milpas* or wherever. This is what happened to my best friend. He was in his *milpa* and the army came upon him and killed him there. This is what happened to him. That's why it frightens you to live there. And that's how I came here. I hardly said goodbye to my family because I left so quickly. I came here.

Since recording this interview, Rodrigo has returned to Guatemala to bring his wife and children to the United States.

Rodrigo's matter-of-fact telling of the personal terror in Guatemala is common in refugee accounts of terrorism. For him and others, the conditions in Guatemala can be described, but the killings and destruction of villages need no stress when told to others. Victor Montejo's *Testimony: Death of a Guatemalan Village* (1987) has a similar style of unexaggerated description: "Before going down to rescue the captives I had learned of the death of one patrol member: the boy of fourteen. . . . It was now two thirty, and the day had begun to cloud over. The bullet-riddled bodies of the dead civil defenders remained where they had fallen. No one, not even the widows, dared to leave the group to weep over the bodies of their husbands" (Montejo 1987:29).

In Rodrigo Antonio's case, the journey through Mexico to California and subsequently to Florida was in itself traumatic. After staying in Mexico City for several months, Rodrigo and a group of four companions (three men and a woman) made their way by train to the U.S. border:

RODRIGO ANTONIO: Well, we got there to Mexicali and we got a ticket for Tijuana. We got to Tijuana and we arrived—how do you say it?—real nervous. There were two women with us as well.

JULIAN ARTURO: Two women with you?

RODRIGO ANTONIO: Yes, two women with their husbands. They were almost dead. When we were on the train, we couldn't even get up. People just walked over us, because we felt so weak for lack of food. When we got to Tijuana, we still had a few pesos. The brother of the *coyote* [a person who brings people across the border for money] found us and we went to his house. There we bathed, ate some eggs, then we went to buy a few beers, so that was the end of that money. That was the last dollar I had; we spent it on beer with that *coyote*. We were in the hands of one of those *coyotes*, in his house.

I went with the *coyote* myself. The *migra* [Immigration and Naturalization Service agents] was there in front of a church. I was really tired and hungry. But when I saw the *migra*, I didn't worry about being tired or hungry, nothing! Thanks to God the church had something, a little park with flowers and everything. That's where I hid.

JULIAN ARTURO: The Mexican *migra* or the United States?

RODRIGO ANTONIO: The United States *migra!* We were in the United States, in Chula Vista, in California. We had already passed on to California. And the *migra* chased me, but thanks to the little park that was in front of the church, I was able to get away. I hid in the flowers and then escaped out the fence to a road that was in front with a lot of cars. I was running behind the *coyote*. We got to another house where they had—how do you call them, those things to carry horses?

JULIAN ARTURO: Horse trailers.

RODRIGO ANTONIO: Horse trailers. An old one was parked

there by the side of the house. The *migra* was still after us, but I was hidden in there, in the trailer. I waited while the *migra* stopped looking. After a while they came back, but I was still hidden in there. Luckily there was a little hill there. That's where I hid myself. I lost the *coyote;* I was all alone; everyone else, including the *coyote,* was gone.

Rodrigo Antonio's story is similar to that of many of the Maya who have come to the United States. California is often the first place that they try to find work, as it is the place where most Mexican *coyotes,* the people who are paid for bringing people across the border, know well. Connover's book *Coyote* (1987) presents a powerful story of what it is like to come across the United States–Mexican border with the help of the *coyotes.*

Rodrigo describes his life in both California and Florida almost as if they were neighboring villages:

RODRIGO ANTONIO: Yes, one of my cousins left when I was in California, the other later. I was by myself. I went up north by myself. The other one stayed in Fort Myers. There a lot of people in Alabama. Too many people. We didn't get anything for our work. It was really hot. Everyone was sweating a lot, even the women who were working there in the sun. We were all sweaty. It was like it was raining; you couldn't even go to the bathroom. And we didn't get anything for it. So after this I went to Michigan.

JULIAN ARTURO: And did you do well there?

RODRIGO ANTONIO: Yes. I went with a woman friend up there to Michigan. We got up there and began picking cherries. We went in June. In one week we made three hundred dollars. "Ay, here there is money," I said. We stayed there for the entire cherry harvest, three weeks. Then we picked apricots, cucumbers. It was really good there. I had work there usually every day. After the apricots, then we picked

apples. Then after the apple harvest, when it gets cold in
November, we came back here again.

JULIAN ARTURO: Where did you go?

RODRIGO ANTONIO: First I spent a few days in Fort Myers;
then I came here to Indiantown.

JULIAN ARTURO: How did you know about Indiantown?

RODRIGO ANTONIO: I had a friend there who had a car, and
he brought me here once to visit some friends who live
here. I knew about Indiantown because when I was living
in Fort Myers I came here to visit now and again. I knew
how it was here. I had friends who gave me a ride here.

One of the first places the Guatemalan Maya can find to live
in Indiantown is in the apartment complexes built to house migrant workers. These apartment buildings are privately owned
but are called "camps" like the farmworker housing found in
the citrus and vegetable farms of the area.

JULIAN ARTURO: Did you come to one of the camps, like
Blue Camp when you came?

RODRIGO ANTONIO: No, I always came here to Seminole
Street. Near the house of Luis. That's where my friend
lives. I picked oranges.

When Rodrigo Antonio returned to Guatemala to find his
family, he found himself conscripted into the "civil patrol," one
of the more burdensome organizations now instituted in many
of the villages such as San Miguel, where Rodrigo was born.
These patrols are made up of local men who are expected to give
up their time to defend the villages from guerrilla soldiers. A
list of every adult man is made in each village, and the men take
turns doing "guard service." Suspicious strangers are reported to
military authorities by these patrols, and often jealousies or old
conflicts between families are settled by a patrol member's

telling the military government that the other party is "subversive." In this way the current system installed by the Guatemalan government to lessen the threat of guerrilla insurgency has been transformed into a means for indulging feuds and personal conflicts. Some men pay others to take their turn at patrol. Many who now work in the United States send back money for years to pay a neighbor or relative to do their patrol duty.

> RODRIGO ANTONIO: When I went back, it had changed a lot. It wasn't at all like it was when the war was going on. Now there is the patrol. You have to be a part of the patrol and not miss a day. When I went back, I had to patrol three times a week. You can't work at all. You have to be on patrol so much that you can't get any work done.
> JULIAN ARTURO: They don't let you work?
> RODRIGO ANTONIO: No. There is no time to work. You have to patrol when it's your turn.
> JULIAN ARTURO: In the camps?
> RODRIGO ANTONIO: No, in our town. We are, as we say, guarding our town. The army is there making sure we do.
> JULIAN ARTURO: So you can't work more than four days a week?
> RODRIGO ANTONIO: Yes, you can't work five days, just four days a week. Most of the time you can only work two or three days a week. You see, that is why the people are so . . . in poverty now. It's because of the patrols, the war. Lots of things have been destroyed.

As we have seen, because political asylum was the most viable strategy for staying in the United States, the Maya like Rodrigo who came here were encouraged to apply for it, even though it was seldom granted. The year or more that it took for cases to go through the appeals process at least gave applicants a period of relative safety when they could legally find jobs and live without fear of deportation. With support from the Indian Law Resource Center in Washington, Jerónimo Camposeco began working with lawyers and other advocates to advance as many political asylum cases as possible through the court systems. The strategy taken by Jerónimo and other advocates was to be forthright about the presence of the Maya in the United States. The filing of political asylum applications provided people with legal status as long as the process of deciding on the individual cases continued. The Maya did not want to remain "undocumented aliens," illegal people. They wanted a chance to maintain their families until it was safe for them to return to Guatemala.

The case of Jerónimo Camposeco is indicative of this process.

ALLAN BURNS: Were you working there in the seventies on a school project or what?

JERONIMO CAMPOSECO: Yes, I was a teacher there in the parochial school teaching little kids. I was teaching them how to write and literacy. And many of these refugees here were my students.

ALLAN BURNS: Were you teaching them to write in Maya as well as in Spanish?

JERONIMO CAMPOSECO: Yes I was, because they don't speak Spanish. I was teaching Maya, in Kanjobal language. It's a Maya language, one of the many Maya languages in Guatemala.

ALLAN BURNS: So you devised an alphabet that could be used.

JERONIMO CAMPOSECO: Yes, we have an alphabet. We are using the modern alphabet of the modern script, but we have to have some changes in the alphabet. We need to learn and then to teach the children. In other words, we teach the children in the modern alphabet, because when they are going to school, they can read in Spanish also. So this is a good help for them. Not only [because to] learn from their own language . . . is more easy, but because if you impose the Spanish since the beginning then. . . . There is a program of the government that is called "Castellanización" that is for the little Indians to learn Spanish before starting school. What I did was teach directly in the Indian language.

ALLAN BURNS: Did the people accept that; did you have a lot of students?

JERONIMO CAMPOSECO: Yes, it was very . . . they accepted that, because they didn't have to do big . . . they didn't have problems to understand the teacher; because they trusted the teacher because the teacher speaks the language. Of course the teacher was another Indian like them.

ALLAN BURNS: You grew up in Jacaltenango, speaking Jacaltec.

JERONIMO CAMPOSECO: Yes, Jacaltenango is a village not too far from San Miguel. We are only divided by two rivers and a mountain. So the Kanjobals go to the market place in Jacaltenango every Sunday carrying their . . . they make, from the maguey fiber, crafts like bags and ropes and all those good things. And also pottery, and also wood for construction. They are very good for those kinds of things like carpentry. . . . So I learned Kanjobal because my father was some kind of instructor also and he had many deals with the Kanjobal.

In the 1970s, Native Americans from New York and Pennsylvania contacted the Maya of Guatemala as part of a pan-Indian movement that crossed national boundaries. Jerónimo and several others from the northwestern highlands were invited to speak and perform marimba music in reservations across the United States and Canada.

ALLAN BURNS: But how did you end up here in Indiantown;
why did you leave Guatemala?

JERONIMO CAMPOSECO: Because I could learn Spanish. I am
an Indian like everybody else. Since I was a kid I helped my
father in the fields, working in the lands and working to
grow milpa and bringing wood to myself. And so I had the
opportunity to go to the school. Later I worked at the National Indian Institute. We were a team of people there, and
we were connected with the North American Indians. And
some of them were working with us in the villages, because
in 1976 was an earthquake, and so some just came to work.
And some of them stayed there after the earthquake until
1980. And this work, for the government, for the paramilitary groups and the death squads, and even the army was
looking for all the people who were working to try to have
a better life in the countryside. Because we are the people
in Guatemala, we are very poor. You know that since colonial times the people in power took our lands—we only
have tiny lands in the mountains, and the good lands are in
the lowlands in the hands of the companies. Exporting all
the products like sugar cane, coffee, bananas, but there is
nothing for our consumption, so I teach the Indians how to
develop their own lands.

ALLAN BURNS: Did the army come for you?

JERONIMO CAMPOSECO: Yes. First of all the army came and
killed some of my friends and my co-workers. Even a North
American Indian was killed by the army; his name was Kayuta Clouds. He was tortured. And because we worked together, the death squads found my name in a letter I sent to
him inviting him to come to Guatemala. And so the American Embassy called to my office saying that I need to be
careful because some people are looking for me because
they found the body of Kay. After that they were looking

for me. So I went to my house and told my wife and my children that I am leaving because the death squads are looking for me. So I escaped to Mexico. My family went to another house. There was a store next to my house. The people there saw three men in a car looking for me, but fortunately my family and I were not there. So I could escape to the United States. And I came to Pennsylvania because there is a place where my friends there, American Indians, farm. And so they gave me refuge there for six months. My family came later, and they joined me in Pennsylvania.

When the Maya of Florida immigrated to the United States in the early 1980s, like many groups of people before them they found the new language, customs, and communities both fascinating and frightening. On the one hand, they found a haven from the disarray of Guatemala, a community that was hospitable to their plight and their work ethic. One woman, Maria Andrés, put it quite succinctly:

MARIA ANDRES: Well, we left Guatemala for the problem that was there, for the war. We wanted to save ourselves in Guatemala, so we came to this land. We looked for each other here in this land. We like living here in this land. Now we don't want to go back to Guatemala.
ALLAN BURNS: What year did you come here?
MARIA ANDRES: In '80 or '81.
ALLAN BURNS: Did you come directly to Indiantown?
MARIA ANDRES: No. We first came to Los Angeles. We came to Los Angeles first. We can't live in our own country, because they are killing a lot of people there. It's because of that. We don't want to die; we want to live in peace, and so we came here. That is the problem that we have.
ALLAN BURNS: And are these your two daughters?

MARIA ANDRES: Yes, one is a niece, but her mother was killed, so she's here with me.

ALLAN BURNS: Did they come with you?

MARIA ANDRES: One of them, yes; the other arrived earlier.

ALLAN BURNS: When did your mother die?

EUGENIA FRANCISCO (the niece): In '79.

ALLAN BURNS: Did she die here or where?

EUGENIA FRANCISCO: In Guatemala. There was an accident.

ALLAN BURNS: And here in the United States, how is life for women?

MARIA ANDRES: No, we don't have problems here. We just want to work here. We just want to live and work here.

ALLAN BURNS: What did you do in Guatemala?

MARIA ANDRES: There in Guatemala, we didn't work. We were in the house, taking care of it and raising our children. That's what we did in our houses.

ALLAN BURNS: Were you making things of clay?

MARIA ANDRES: No, it was others who did that. Where we lived we didn't. We made food for those who worked, the *campesinos.* That is what we were doing. Now, we have to go and look for work elsewhere, well, because here there isn't any work. We won't be able to work anymore here. We'll leave and then we'll return here again after the work.

ALLAN BURNS: Where will you go?

MARIA ANDRES: To New York.

ALLAN BURNS: To New York?

MARIA ANDRES: All of us, the whole family will go. We are taking the number of the center here with us in case our application comes up and they have to call us for an appointment. If they do, we'll come by plane for the appointment for political asylum. That's what we're going to do.

ALLAN BURNS: What do you need here in Indiantown?

MARIA ANDRES: If the president would let us, we would buy a little land here so we could live better.

Maria Andrés and others from Guatemala came to Florida and found jobs, first in the citrus groves, later in construction and the service industries. They found their friends who had fled several years earlier, and some went back to bring wives and children. With the passing of years, their children learned English and some went to college. Others moved away from Indiantown to see other parts of the United States and to see what it means to be a Maya American.

The narratives of the violence of Guatemala, the flight to the United States, and the difficulties of staying in the United States legally now make up a new oral history among the Maya of the United States. The narratives are not just stories of a journey, but are at the intersection of personal history and political adaptation. People like Maria Andrés who are not practiced in public speaking have had to talk about events that are personally tragic and that run counter to the prevailing beliefs of U.S. citizens and immigration authorities. Their stories are met with incredulity, an incredulity often fueled by the legal expectation of precision with regard to dates and locations. The narratives have been honed through interaction with lawyers working for political asylum, but even when dates and places are precisely given, new challenges are brought forward. Sometimes it is the challenge of time itself: after a few years threats and persecution are thought to disappear, and dangers experienced a few years ago are not seen as real today. Sometimes the challenge is to the veracity of the asylum seekers, as when an immigration hearing judge doubts that a gentle Maya person could recall such tragic events in a voice without emotion.

THREE

LIFE CRISIS AND RITUAL

Maya people smile when they translate the name of Indiantown into Spanish. *El Pueblo de los Indios*, or "The Town of the Indians," has indeed become a population center as well as a symbolic center of Kanjobal Maya culture in exile. Local residents, overwhelmed and sometimes frustrated by the immigration of so many people from Guatemala, say that the name should be changed to "Guatemala town." In Indiantown, the Maya are visible: there they make up the majority of the migrant workers in the area along with a large number of Mexicans and Mexicans Americans, African Americans, and Haitians.

Indiantown demands new forms of adaptation and organization for the Maya. Family ceremonies such as baptisms and weddings provide a framework within which to organize small groups of people into bonds of ritual friendship. Larger events such as the yearly celebration of the patron saint of San Miguel Acatán provide a second field where new ways of organizing for survival in the United States can be developed. Voluntary associations and clubs have also become common in the community as the Maya and other Guatemalans have become more numerous. These voluntary associations are especially important in a small community such as Indiantown, as they provide a recognizable and comprehensible structure for the non-Maya residents. An ethnic or nationality-based "club" allows members of other associations, such as the Kiwanis, PTA, or county government, to meet with the new Maya of Indiantown in routine ways; the president of the PTA, for example, knows to call the president of the CORN-Maya association. Without this and other associations, the Maya of the community would become an isolated enclave.

Indiantown is some twenty miles inland from the Atlantic coast of Florida, situated near the edge of Lake Okeechobee in the rich citrus, cattle, and winter vegetable zone of Florida. As we will see in more detail in Chapter Four, it is a crossroads town with one stop light, intersected by a north-south highway running alongside of Lake Okeechobee and an east-west road that connects the town with the county seat of Stuart, Florida. Like so many towns in the agriculture zone of Florida, Indiantown has a grocery store, several convenience stores, a post office, and a few businesses situated along the main highway. The southern end of town is called "Indiantown proper," while the northern part, where African Americans and most farmworkers live, is called "Booker Park." The town is not segregated by race or ethnicity as much as it is by economics. Those who can move out of the Booker Park area do so in favor of the relatively safe "uptown" area.

Every week more Maya arrive. Miguel Antonio, his wife Dominga Miguel, and their two children crossed the border into Arizona, aided not by *coyotes* but by Native Americans who recognized a bond of culture between themselves and the Maya of Guatemala. According to the Antonios, the Native Americans of Arizona charge half what the Mexican *coyotes* charge to bring the Maya across the border. Still, it is dangerous: "Those Indian people drink; they smuggle drugs. Sometimes they are drunk and high on cocaine at the same time when we were crossing the desert. They are really crazy."

Once in Indiantown, the Maya continue their quest for safety. One of the first places people find to live is in cardboard boxes or old buses and automobiles. There the rent is cheap; twenty-five dollars a week for an old bus is a good price. But it is better to live in one of the "camps," or converted apartment buildings rented to farmworkers. At least there neighbors can help out in case of emergency. In one of these buildings, called "Blue Camp," rooms are divided by curtains so that two or three families can pay high rent to absentee landlords. Another, "White Camp," consists of a set of tiny houses on the edge of town. For several years there was an apartment house called "Yellow Camp." Yellow Camp had a more infamous name, "the Roach Palace," before publicity forced the owners to clean it up. Finally the building was razed.

Life in these camps is crowded. Blue Camp, for example, looks from the outside like a two-story motel or apartment complex. The parking lot is usually muddy and full of potholes, with a large garbage dumpster in front. Along with cars and vans with license plates from many states is an occasional school bus. Sometimes a church from a nearby community sends a portable classroom where English classes are given. Bicycles are pulled up alongside doorways, and lively Latin music can be heard from several radios. During the week most people in the camp are at work, but on weekend afternoons it is common to encounter groups of young men standing outside doorways talking, sometimes drinking beer. People are friendly, but still wary of strangers. Evictions, arrests, and immigration checks are common.

Inside an apartment, the most notable sensation is one of heat. Southern Florida is very warm, and the inland area of Indiantown lacks the cooling ocean breezes of the coast. Daytime highs in the nineties and up to a hundred and nighttime lows in the eighties are common much of the year.

The apartments are made up of two rooms and a bathroom, with a "kitchenette" in one of the rooms, often located near the door. The kitchenette contains a small stove, a sink, and a counter. A few apartments have refrigerators. Windows are often closed, especially at night, for security and because of the prevalence of mosquitos. The rooms are crowded, as two or three families often share floor space. Infectious diseases such as tuberculosis, dysentery, and others easily transmitted in crowded conditions are common. While Maya people are extremely clean, they fight an uphill battle against the conditions found in the apartments.

A curtain is sometimes hung from the ceiling to separate one family's sleeping pallet from another's. The walls are bare, except for a few calendars or a wall hanging from Guatemala. Women usually arise at four or five o'clock in the morning to begin making tortillas and other food for the men who work in the fields. The early morning hours are busy as people pack up food, get rides to work sites, and prepare for the day. During the day some women work at a local textile cooperative, some go to the fields, and others baby-sit for their neighbors. The unpredictable job market leaves many people idle each day, so some wander around town looking for work.

In the camps life is dangerous. People have been murdered for not paying a *coyote* the amount owed for crossing the border. Robberies are common. It is well known that Maya men and women carry their wages with them and seldom use banks to guard their money. This, coupled with their short stature and gentle nature, makes the Maya easy targets. The local paper in Indiantown often has articles about homicides and other crimes against the Guatemalan Maya:

> The identity of a Latin man found stabbed several
> times . . . early Saturday morning had not been released at
> press time Tuesday.

Martin County Sheriff Sgt. Billy Chase said that [the man] was discovered dead near a chicken house. Deputies were called at 6:44 A.M. and found the victim stabbed several times in the chest and his throat cut.

The man was described as between 19 to 23 years old, about 5 feet 5 inches, and weighing 110 pounds. He wore a red, white and black striped sports shirt, blue jeans and sneakers. . . . The murder is still being investigated. (Indiantown *News*, Jan. 28, 1987)

White residents of the town find jobs in schools, agricultural service industries, and a military helicopter factory south of the community. Other residents, including African Americans, Haitians, Puerto Ricans, Mexicans, and Guatemalans, have multiple occupational strategies. When farm work is available, it is sought after. When it is not, landscape work, day labor in construction, child care, salvaging, and other informal sector jobs are pursued.

After a while, when work has been plentiful and they have learned the geography of the town, some Maya may be able to rent a house. Once a house is rented, however, pressure to take in several more families of relatives, friends, and recent arrivals from Guatemala is strong. Once I came upon a vanload of eleven Guatemalans who were on their way to Indiantown. I asked if they had relatives or friends there. They didn't, but they had the name of someone who had a house in the town. They knew they could stay there a week or so until they found a place of their own.

One way that people adapt to this new and sometimes frightening life is through personal and community ceremonies. Life crisis events such as births, baptisms, marriages, and funerals are times when activities that are familiar parts of life in Guatemala can be adapted to life in the United States. Baptisms are especially important in this regard, since baptisms include the naming of godparents, and godparenthood provides a social network in the community. Godparenthood in Guatemala and Indiantown places an emphasis on the ties between the parents of a child and the godparents. This is in contrast to an emphasis on the godparent-godchild relationship as defined in Catholic liturgy. The Spanish terms *compadre* and *comadre* refer to these bonds established between the adults through baptism.

The use of baptisms or marriages to create networks of *compadrazgo* bonds is an efficient strategy for creating a social structure in a place like Indiantown. Several groups have formed in the community based on a combination of kinship, godparenthood ties, and religious affiliation. One group consists of many of the first arrivals to the community who were active in cooperatives and educational reform programs in Guatemala. Another group centers on a onetime store owner from the town of San Miguel who is a staunch Catholic and who has worked hard to better the school system for Guatemalan children. A third is made up of people who converted to Seventh Day Adventism and do not participate in traditional Catholic activities such as baptisms or marriages. The workings of this network can be seen in a description of how a baptism organizes family and friends, in this case the baptism of the daughter of Jacinta and Domingo Andrés.

Jacinta looks into the lens of the video camera, smiles, and nervously takes a breath before starting to talk. She and her husband, Domingo, have asked us to videotape their daughter's baptism so that the family can remember what it was like when they came to Florida. The Maya who fled Guatemala for Mexico and the United States have quickly adapted to audio and video cassettes for communication. Audio tapes—recorded in Maya and containing news of government programs and guerrilla activity and family information—line the closets of many Maya. Now that video recorders are within the reach of many refugees, videotape has also become an important resource in the community. Weddings, baptisms, and community festivals are regularly recorded. One of the ways that I began working with the community was by offering to videotape celebrations such as marriages, baptisms, and festivals.

Jacinta and Domingo were health promoters in Guatemala. Domingo left Guatemala first, in 1985, and it took almost a year for Jacinta to join him after he came to the United States. I had met Domingo when he and other Guatemalan Maya came to my office at the University of Florida one day to see me. Domingo had been planning to go back to Guatemala to get his wife and child now that he had found a place in Indiantown. He asked if I could write a letter on their behalf to the U.S. embassy in Guatemala City. I promptly did so. I mentioned in the letter that the presence of two health promoters would be a tremendous help to the Maya community in Indiantown. As Maria Miralles points out in her book on women's health in the community, *A Matter of Life and Death* (1989), one of the greatest problems with the influx of Maya refugees to the small unincorporated community of Indiantown is the lack of communication between the Guatemalan Maya and the health care institutions.

Domingo returned to the highlands with my letter and others in hand. The embassy did not grant them a visa, but he brought his wife back anyway, along with their two daughters, the younger of whom, Carmen, had been born in his absence. The baptism was a chance to express his gratitude for being able to bring his family together again.

The baptism begins in the morning of this Saturday in August with the ceremony at the church, and it continues into the early morning of the next day. The religious part of the ceremony takes place at a small Catholic church where a Spanish-speaking priest performs the fifteen-minute baptism rite. The church is empty except for Jacinta and Domingo and the god-parents for Carmen, Jerónimo and his wife Anna. The child is held over a baptismal font, and the priest pours water over her head. Carmen cries, and the priest smiles as he ends the cere-mony. He then talks informally to the parents and godparents, remarking that the child is now "his" in that she belongs to the church as a new Christian. He shows genuine affection for the child, in part because Jacinta and Domingo are devout Catholics and their example of regular church attendance is important in the community. The naming of godparents itself is a way of cementing the bonds between Jacinta and Domingo and other families of the community. Jerónimo and Anna, for example, are godparents to many of the new arrivals, forming one of the major groups in the community through common bonds of kinship and baptism.

After the church ceremony the families and friends go to a restaurant to celebrate the baptism. The only fancy restaurant in town is in a "bed and breakfast" hotel that caters to out-of-town tourists and local residents and is consequently seldom visited by the Maya. The food is good, but some of the dishes, such as the peanut butter pie, seem strange.

Jacinta and Domingo live in a rental house in the "uptown" part of Indiantown. It is a small, cement block home of about nine hundred square feet. In the afternoon they work at home to prepare for the baptism "fiesta." Chickens are cooked in a cream sauce, soda pop is bought from the supermarket in town, and paper plates are arranged on several card tables put out in the living room for the guests. A marimba is brought over from one of the other houses, and a few men set it up against one wall in the living room and begin playing.The marimba—a five-foot-long xylophone instrument—takes up one side of the room, which has a Maya child's ceremonial dress and a sash tacked to the wall as the only decoration. By six in the evening, people start arriving. It is very hot, both inside and out, as temperatures in August are in the high nineties and hundreds during the day and in the high eighties at night. The ferocious mosquitos outside the house are biting the men who are standing around drinking a few beers. Inside several women sit on the couch in front of the marimba; others help Jacinta and Domingo serve the food.

People continue to arrive throughout the evening. The marimba music continues unabated all night with only a few breaks as one player or another is spelled by another musician. The Maya women are bashful and seldom dance during the evening. As a result, the Maya men dance many dances with Jacinta, and with her *comadre* Anna. Most people are content to listen and watch. Children are present, and take turns watching younger brothers and sisters as they toddle around the house.

By one in the morning there are only fifteen people left. Most families have gone home with their children, and the group that remains is mostly men. Domingo walks over to his other daughter, four-year-old Catrina, picks her up, and begins dancing. Catrina has not recovered from the spinal meningitis she contracted in Guatemala. Domingo holds her and dances slowly to the marimba music in Maya style, moving his feet slowly and keeping his upper body straight. Catrina smiles slightly as Domingo continues to dance.

Domingo and Jacinta have reason to dance with Catrina. When they crossed the border this summer with both children, they were picked up by the police and were about to be taken to the border patrol to be deported. When the police saw Catrina, however, they realized that she was about to die, so they rushed her to a hospital. The doctors were amazed that she was still alive but said that there was nothing they could do for her. They released Catrina to her parents, who continued on their way to the haven of Indiantown. Their daughter Catrina saved them from being deported back to Guatemala and from the dangers there that they had escaped.

At three o'clock in the morning, one-year-old Carmen is still somehow awake, being passed from Jacinta's father Francisco to Julian Arturo, a student at the University of Florida, while her parents continue to serve food and drink to the group of people who are still at the party. The kitchen is hot from the big pots of boiled chicken. As Domingo continues to pass out soft drinks and beer, an older man turns to me and says, "Domingo is really a good person. Look at him attending to the guests this late." The four men playing the marimba have been playing since seven o'clock in the evening and yet do not look tired. Whenever one player decides to take a break and get something to eat or drink, another musician steps into his place. Their expression is serious: playing the marimba is a sincere activity, and musicians wait until their breaks to smile and laugh with the others at the party.

A marimba player starts singing, *"Ya me voy, ya me voy, porque yo no soy de aquí. Soy de un pueblo muy lejano, yo soy de San Miguel Acatán,"* in English, "I'm going, I'm going, because I am not from here. I'm from a town so far away, I'm from San Miguel Acatán." The song has become something of a theme melody in Indiantown over the last few years. It is played and sung at community fiestas such as the feast day of San Miguel, Christmas, and harvest celebrations. Domingo has added several more verses to the song, incorporating the other ethnic groups into the community in the lyrics, and sings the extended version at church services. Tonight, though, the sparse verses of the original are sung in refrain to the marimba music.

Finally, about three-thirty in the morning the marimba players stop. They have been playing for close to ten hours. The people who remain are the godparents; Jacinta's father, Francisco; Julian Arturo; and I. Julian and I have videotaped the ceremony, the dinner, the dancing, and now, weary after over eighteen hours of ceremony, we stand in an informal circle with the family members. There is enough tape left for a few final comments.

Jacinta is shy, and only after some prompting from the others does she speak in Spanish: "I just hope that she is able to advance a little more than we have," she says, "advance in society, in education, in culture, in life. I want her to remember all the people who were here tonight."

Jeronimo begins to speak in Kanjobal Mayan. He then switches to Spanish and finally to English:

> It is important that our goddaughter Carmen remember this night. Because I know that she is going to be a leader of her people. Her people have suffered so much. She should remember her people, her language, and her customs. I just hope she is able to keep her customs and remain strong, not like other groups that have come here, because the discrimination here is the worst I have ever seen. To overcome this she will have to have a strong family and culture. Her home in Guatemala is no longer a place for her.

The Maya refugees in Indiantown have organized themselves to make their voices heard in the community. The Kanjobal Maya held positions of leadership in their villages in Guatemala. The system of shared religious and political offices, the civil-religious hierarchy, has been described by Wagley (1949), Nash (1967), Tedlock (1982), and many others who have studied the highland Maya of Guatemala and Mexico. Traditional political organization in Maya communities included offices, or *cargos*, that were held for a year. These offices often included religious service like caring for a saint's image and sponsoring a fiesta, as well as political service like being a mayor or a local police officer. Each office had increasing responsibility and prestige. The hierarchy offered the means of advancement for families. As an officeholder gained more experience, he was able to advance to the most important political and religious positions in the community, the *principales*, or elders (La Farge 1947).

In the 1970s this old system of community organization was joined by others: agricultural and educational cooperatives, craft guilds, and labor unions. Likewise, the military programs in the 1980s in Guatemala brought another kind of organization to the Maya: that of the forced drafting of youngsters and of political control based on violence and terror. Today, political office in many Maya communities in Guatemala is held by local men who serve under the guidance of the Interinstitutional Coordination structures created by the military after the resettlement programs of the mid-1980s (Manz 1988).

Indiantown is a difficult place to develop leadership and organization for people like the Maya. Their work is physically exhausting. After working ten to twelve hours a day in the fields, few people have the energy for going to meetings or even for talking. But still, some political self-sufficiency and empowerment has taken hold.

The community has organized itself around several issues, some of which have cut across the sharp divisions that exist among the Maya. Some Maya are Catholic, while many others are traditionalists, or belong to the Seventh-Day Adventists and other Protestant denominations. Some Maya sided with the Guatemalan government during the period of massive violence; others sided with the guerilla movement; many people switched sides, allying themselves with whichever side seemed less abusive and more likely to be in control.

Political offices in Indiantown are not available to the Maya immigrants. As an unincorporated community, the town is governed by a county commission in the coastal county seat of Stuart. The large population of the coast as compared to the area around Indiantown makes it difficult for anyone from Indiantown to be elected to the county commission. Some Indiantown residents are elected to the commission, but only those who are established residents, not migrant workers and refugees.

There are a few positions that could be considered locally important. There are, for example, offices in voluntary associations such as the chamber of commerce or the local Kiwanis club. The Maya are not members of these organizations, both because of their legal status and because of the kinds of work they do. Church positions are another arena where leadership in the community can be fostered. The Seventh-Day Adventists and the Catholic churches have both sponsored Kanjobal Maya as leaders of choirs, youth groups, and other activities.

Carmen's baptism is an example of building networks from the personal level of family ceremony. The broadest form of community organizing among the Maya in Indiantown takes place through the association created to carry on the patronal festival of San Miguel each September. Marking the end of summer migrant work in the North and the beginning of the Florida harvest season, the fiesta is an important event. It also has tremendous emotional and cultural appeal for the Maya. It is a time when several thousand Maya come together and speak their own language, catch up on changes here and back in Guatemala, and plan for the future.

Beginning in 1982 as a small Sunday event that was more religious than social, the fiesta has grown in size each year. It now lasts three days, drawing people from as far away as Oregon, California, and even Guatemala. In addition to the procession of the image of St. Michael and the mass on Sunday, the fiesta features soccer games, dances, a market, and other cultural events.

The fiesta attracts several thousand people each year, the majority of them Maya. It opens on Friday evening with a "cultural night" at seven in the evening. Crowds of people stand around a stage area where a few floodlights have been hung from trees to illuminate the huge banner of St. Michael the Archangel that a volunteer from the Catholic church painted several years ago. The marimba is set up to one side. The marimba moves throughout the weekend to different activity areas, serving to focus attention on the fiesta's important events. On Saturday it is set up next to the soccer field and on Sunday it is moved into the church.

The cultural night begins with a welcome speech by the organizers of the fiesta and the introduction of visitors from Guatemala or perhaps a priest once active in Guatemala. Some years, awards are handed out for community service. Local musicians are asked to play, and sometimes dances from the societies of Central America are performed by representatives from different countries. Maya school children have practiced their activities for several weeks. These include walking onto the stage with signs stating the names of the departments of Guatemala, short speeches, and dances.

Finally the queens of the festival, each escorted by a young man, are called up one after another. The queens wear elaborately embroidered *huipiles,* or blouses, and handwoven skirts, often imported from Guatemala especially for the occasion. The young men wear white shirts with red bandannas and new slacks. On stage each queen is given a sash with her name and the name of the group she is representing, and is crowned by either the local priest or a visiting priest. Each queen then gives a short speech welcoming people to the fiesta.

After this, music continues, either in the form of the marimba or a hybrid band of marimba, electric guitar, and drums. A few young people dance to the music while several hundred people stand around in a huge semicircle. The people in the crowd watch, talk to friends, and sometimes drink.

On Saturday of the fiesta the principal activity is the soccer matches. Teams from Hispanic communities throughout the farmworker region of south Florida compete in a tournament that lasts all of Saturday and into Sunday. In addition to the soccer tournament, food concessions and arts and crafts booths are set up on the fiesta grounds. Haitian, Mexican, Puerto Rican, and Guatemalan foods are available. The fiesta organizers sell T-shirts with a Guatemalan logo such as a quetzal bird, the phrase "Fiesta of San Miguel," and the year printed on them. Some consumer items such as televisions and radios are raffled off in the late afternoon. During one fiesta, a number of men went to a K-Mart discount store and bought masks and performed the Dance of the Elders to the marimba band in the afternoon. That practice was not continued, however, though it was thoroughly enjoyed by participants. In the early 1990s, costumes were imported from Guatemala so that the Dance of the Conquest could be performed. Like tourists everywhere, many Maya people have bought cameras and video camcorders, so another activity of the fiesta is taking pictures and recording the events on videotape. A dance is sometimes held on Saturday night. Two groups of musicians take turns playing for the dance: the traditional Maya marimba band and a more modern Mexican-American rock band.

Sunday morning begins with a procession of the image of Saint Michael from the church, around the festival grounds, and back to the church. The song discussed earlier, "San Miguel," is sung by Jacinto Andrés over the church loudspeaker as the procession marches around the church grounds. Soccer teams, the queens, visitors, and anyone else who cares to, marches in the procession. When the procession returns to the church, the mass of Saint Michael is performed. The church itself has been decorated with garlands of woven pine needles, traditional Maya textiles, and banners. The mass includes a baptism, often with as many as twenty children being baptized at once.

After the mass a meal is served that has been prepared by one of the fiesta committees. In the afternoon the soccer matches continue and the winners of the soccer tournament receive their trophies. There is no definite end to the fiesta, as people wander off throughout the day on Sunday.

The overall tone of the fiesta is one of quiet sociability. Hours and hours are spent standing or sitting around talking with friends, and the different events such as the mass, the cultural evening, or the soccer matches are not given a great deal of attention. Outsiders are often somewhat confused, as they expect an event with strong focal points and hundreds of joyful people. What they find are groups of people quietly smiling and talking in Maya and events going on that may be participated in or ignored, depending on individual taste. But for the Maya, this quiet, gentle style of participation is the key to the cultural importance of the fiesta. It is first and foremost their fiesta, and their participation in it is an indication of their own identity.

The fiesta is organized through a steering committee made up of representatives from the major family groups in Indiantown as well as representatives of the other nearby communities that have a significant Maya population, such as Lake Worth and Okeechobee. The fiesta committee received its impetus through the Catholic church in Indiantown under the pastorship of a strong advocate priest, Frank O'Loughlin. After several years of fiestas, its structure has evolved to include subcommittees to handle entertainment, sports, cultural activities, and food. This structure serves to give leadership experience in a way fitting with the traditional *cargo* of Maya society. Newcomers to Indiantown may be asked to take charge of the artisan market or help organize the soccer tournament and in that way use leadership skills on a small scale. In succeeding years, these same people may be asked to serve on more important committees.

There is an important difference, however, between this kind of organizing when it takes place in Guatemala and the same activity in Indiantown. In Guatemala the fiesta is a manifestation of the indigenous political structure. In the United States, organizing the fiesta is an act of social and cultural dependency.

> ALLAN BURNS: How has the fiesta changed? What is different between the fiesta in San Miguel and the fiesta here in Florida?
>
> CARLOS RIVAS: Here we are the guests. We have to ask for permission to use the field, to hold the soccer matches, to hold the fiesta. There in Guatemala, we *were* the community. We gave permission for the fireworks, for the dances. Here the sheriff doesn't even speak Spanish. There, one of us was appointed sheriff.

Still, the fiesta committee is an important part of Maya organization in Indiantown. The fiesta is a successful public event that draws Maya and other migrant workers from all over Florida and nearby states. Newspaper accounts bring some attention to the community. Consequently, its organizers achieve a measure of local fame, and the community as a whole gains positive publicity.

Over the years since the first San Miguel festival was held in Indiantown, several conflicts have arisen. The conflicts reflect the changes that have occurred in the community as it has evolved from a refugee community to a more settled Maya center. One conflict arose between the official church leadership and the Maya. The fact that Father O'Loughlin's church was the site of the festival was not appreciated by many of the Maya who were not Catholic. While many of the Protestant

Maya nevertheless came to the festival, many Seventh-Day Adventists stayed away. Likewise, leadership in festival organizing committees was generally limited to practicing Catholics, which effectively kept many people from participating. These problems were exacerbated when a new priest was sent to the community who encouraged the festival, but asked for funds to pay for the use of the church grounds. The next year, the organizers decided to use the county park, which was located at the edge of the community, rather than the more central church grounds. This move away from the church grounds reflected a structural change in the Maya's relationship with Indiantown, a move toward a wider legitimacy. While the church was the first sponsor of the Maya in the community, it was not representative enough to sustain the community by itself.

The program for the fiesta reveals many of the changes that are occurring in the community. Advertisers include food vendors from the other ethnic groups in the community. The soccer tournament, which has become a large part of the festival, draws teams from farmworker communities throughout South Florida. The teams are organized along ethnic lines, some teams being made up of Mexican farmworkers, and others Guatemalan. The division of the teams even extends to local communities in Guatemala; one team from West Palm Beach is made up of several Jacaltec Maya whereas the Indiantown team is made up of Kanjobal Maya.

The queens are elected to represent specific groups. One represents workers, another the Kanjobal soccer team, and a third the fiesta itself. The speech given by each of the queens during the cultural evening must be delivered in Kanjobal, Spanish, and then English. The fiesta gives these women the chance to practice their skills in front of a crowd of people and to see the value of multilingualism.

The speech given at a recent fiesta by Juana Martin, one of

the queens, who had just received a two-year community college degree, provides a glimpse into the changing ideology of the Maya. Her speech was given first in Kanjobal and then in English. In the English version, given below, the queen stresses that, because few people know the Kanjobal, the festival attempts to reach out to other people, especially those who do not speak Spanish. She wants to help win recognition for the Kanjobal presence in the United States and she wants people to understand that, although they are at times invisible migrant workers, the Maya are a people with a heritage and a culture.

Good evening ladies and gentlemen. We the Kanjobal people from San Miguel Acatán, Guatemala country, welcome you to this San Miguel festival.

We appreciate that you are here in this special moment for us. As you know, we have arrived in the United States since a long time ago. This is the third time that we celebrate this festival. We haven't done this before because of special circumstances. But now we got help from a lot of people from San Miguel. They have been doing this festival. This is hard work for us. We really love to see each one of the people from San Miguel in this town.

We feel proud because of our heritage. But it is hard for each one of us to show who we are and where we come from.

We feel that each of you think we don't have anything to do with Nature, but we do in this country.

We want to show each one of you who are not Spanish speakers that we love each other. We want to be friends with you here.

We want you to believe that we are in the United States. We want to show you our tradition, our custom. We love you here and we know that you love us here too. You are

welcome in this San Miguel festival. We hope that you enjoy and we hope that you have a good time here.

As we have seen, the fiesta of San Miguel is also a time when
children are baptized in the Catholic church. As in many Spanish and Spanish-American communities, to be baptized during
the festival is highly regarded. Not only will the child's baptism
day be the same as that of the patron saint of the community,
but because visiting clergy are often invited to the festival, a
child can be baptized by a high-ranking Catholic priest. Baptisms are also done at the festival because it is much easier for
the godparents of choice to attend during the days of the festival
than at other times of the year, especially if they have been
working in the migrant stream.

The festival articulates these private, family connections of
godparenthood with the migrant work cycle, the history and
memories of San Miguel in Guatemala, and the emerging system of leadership in the community. Past festival leaders, either
committee organizers or the queens, have moved on to jobs
within the local Catholic diocese, within the county government, and within private businesses such as small shops in
Indiantown.

Associations began to appear soon after the Maya arrived in
Indiantown as ways of connecting the refugee experience with
the community. The Indian Law Resource Center and American Friends Service Committee lawyers working with the Maya
asylum seekers pushed the Maya to develop leadership. Meetings were regularly held with those Maya who knew Spanish, in
an effort to organize the community to defend itself and to learn
about immigration law.

One such organization was the Kanjobal Association. Begun
in 1985, it had an initial membership of over three hundred
people. The association directed its efforts toward legal referral

and education, especially as immigration and political asylum policy began to change. The Immigration Reform and Control Act of 1986, known generally as "IRCA," had just come into effect. The Maya needed information about whether they might qualify under the farmworker provision of this law.

Likewise, many Maya had applied for political asylum upon their arrival. New immigrants to the community had to be notified of the procedures for filing asylum applications and what to expect in the ensuing court hearings. Many "street-corner" notaries in South Florida suddenly appeared to fill the vacuum created by a lack of organizations that could complete political asylum papers. The new notary businesses filled out forms quickly for as little as twenty-five dollars and as much as three hundred dollars. They promised that political asylum application would provide a temporary work permit, which was indeed the case, but the flood of such applications worried the lawyers who had been working with the Maya for several years. The applications they worked with were painstakingly documented, and the fear of persecution and murder was a major part of each case. Applications that were filled out by notaries were not documented and had little chance of passing the scrutiny of immigration judges.

The Kanjobal Association was successful, but short-lived. The issue of immigrant status, while very important, was not enough to keep people coming to meetings after they had heard what they needed to know. Maya people have continued to come into the community. Those who arrived applied for political asylum through notaries and were assured of at least twelve months of asylum while their cases were processed. This, added to the tremendous caseload of the American Friends Service Committee, meant that these quicker political asylum applications soon outnumbered the legitimate ones. The Maya had also learned that political asylum was an empty hope: only a handful of Guatemalans have achieved asylum in the past eight years, even though thousands have applied. (The 1990s saw a second chance for political asylum, as noted in Chapter One, as the American Baptist Churches Supreme Court decision re-opened thousands of Guatemalan political asylum cases.)

The Kanjobal Association operated for slightly more than a year. While it was not sustained as an ongoing mechanism for community identity and development, it did, like the festival, provide opportunities for the Maya to meet with lawyers and paralegal workers and functioned as an institution for information for a short time.

A more durable association was formed under the name CORN-Maya, an acronym derived from Comité de Refugiados Maya. CORN-Maya began in 1983 as an advocacy organization composed of Guatemalan Maya and several anthropologists active in documenting the violence in the northwestern highlands. Soon after its inception, CORN-Maya representatives went to Los Angeles, and founded a similar group there known as IXIM, the Maya word for corn. Both CORN-Maya and IXIM have community development and advocacy as their aim. CORN-Maya's goals are conveniently summarized in a description written by Jerónimo Camposeco in one of the organization's educational bulletins:

> [CORN-Maya's] goals are cultural unity, legal assistance, people's human rights advocacy, and public education that could bring the point of view of the people who suffer in Central America. Since colonial times we lost our self determination, but since 1980 the Guatemala Maya have been facing the predicament of political isolation and cultural destruction. A group of Kanjobal Mayan people escaped to the United States and are telling our account of our tragedy to the American people that is a little different from the official information.

We are an Indian Nation in Exile. Dynamic cultural conservation is a key issue for us to continue and practice our way of life in order to live here with dignity and self-sufficiency as we survive the culture shock of a new society. Let's work together and build the survival of a people who are in danger: the Maya. We want to struggle along with our brothers and sisters of the Indian Nations in North America for our rights and respect as people. We are a new Indian Nation in this land. Our mutual support is the key to gaining our freedom. Just as the eagle is sacred to the people of the United States, the multicolored Quetzal is sacred to us.

CORN-Maya has gained support for political asylum case preparation, especially when political asylum was a viable strategy for the Maya who came in the mid-1980s. With help from the University of Florida Department of Anthropology, CORN-Maya has also secured a folk arts apprenticeship grant from the state of Florida to develop marimba classes for Maya teenagers who have little to do in the migrant community but hang around people's houses. The organization has also been successful in achieving external funding for emergency food banks, work and institutional referral, and community development.

CORN-Maya gained nonprofit status in the state of Florida and also was able to achieve tax-exempt status under Internal Revenue statutes. While the official recognition of CORN-Maya provided much-needed official legitimacy for fund-raising and grant management, the association faced problems that were similar to those of other organizations of the Maya in the United States. Without an operating budget, CORN-Maya relied on donations, grants, and volunteer help from students. Students from Vanderbilt University and the University of Florida worked to support the organization while a few Maya volunteered their services as association directors and officers. But to many people in the Maya community, CORN-Maya was perceived as a scheme by a few people to "get rich" by charging for filling out immigration forms, receiving money from the U.S. government, and receiving grants from other unknown sources. As a result, envy and mistrust developed within the community about the activities of the organization. Some members of the Guatemalan community resented the "Indian" identification of CORN-Maya, arguing that there are now many people in the community from Guatemala who are not "Indian." The traditional shame at being called an "Indian" in Guatemala, coupled with the association of the "Indians" with the guerrilla insurgency, helps explain why this group did not want to be known as an indigenous association. Meetings were held in the early 1990s. Accusations of fraud and misrepresentation of the community and personal invectives were shouted back and forth. Some pushing and shoving broke out at one meeting. Finally, a solution was reached in the early 1990s when a second group was organized and new officers of CORN-Maya were elected.

CORN-Maya's directors were faced with a problem of greater proportions. As the organization became known as a point of referral in the community, it was pressed with meeting two demands. The first was the demand by the press, the churches, and other agencies for someone to act as a "spokesperson" for the Maya community. Every reporter who came to town, every student interested in the Maya, every social service or health worker who needed to talk to someone in the Maya community, was referred to the director of CORN-Maya. At the same time, CORN-Maya faced demands from the Maya of Indiantown for someone to serve their personal needs. CORN-Maya was the place to call if one was in Guatemala or somewhere between Guatemala and Florida. In one month alone the long-distance charges for the office came to over five hundred dollars. CORN-Maya was also the place where one could go for emergency housing, for messages, for leads on jobs, for marital counseling, for legal assistance, for help in completing income tax forms, and for the immigration assistance that was the original intent of the association.

Exhausted after two years of service as director of CORN-Maya, Jacinto Andrés relinquished his position and went to work in the construction industry:

ALLAN BURNS: What happened this past year? What can the association do in the future?

JACINTO ANDRES: You know, my house isn't even mine. My family and I pay rent on that place, but over half of it is taken up with CORN-Maya activities: the marimba, the office, the files. But even worse is the fact that I get no rest. I get calls at three in the morning from people all over the country looking for their family or friends in Indiantown. The sheriff comes by at midnight because someone got in an accident or was robbed and is in the hospital. People come by looking for their husbands or for their children. I get no sleep, because I work all day for the community and then at night I have to answer the telephone and take care of these emergencies. My wife and children are affected by all of this. We can't help everybody. CORN-Maya has no money, yet people always come by looking for help. And they need it! People arrive here without food, without a place to sleep. What can we do? We have to help them, but I can't go on as the director.

Jacinto had come to the community to help, to be a leader in the best way he could. But the pressure of community demands, both internal and external, was too great. Working twelve hours a day in construction was preferable to facing the overwhelming needs of those Maya who continued to arrive in the community in need of help.

Some of the Maya refugees have been in Florida since 1983,

although most have been here only a year or so. They are a refugee group that has a high turnover in Indiantown. Some leave for California, where a large Guatemalan community lives in the city of Los Angeles. Others head north to join a few families scattered throughout New England and Canada. Still others make their way back to Mexico and Guatemala, hoping against hope that things will be different and they can pick up their lives again.

For every person who leaves, there are several who arrive in Indiantown. The Maya are now the dominant ethnic group in the community, ahead of Mexicans, Haitians, and other Central Americans. But young Maya Americans born here in the United States and attending the public schools have few avenues open for drawing on their own cultural heritage. Events like Carmen's baptism and the fiesta of Saint Michael link the personal family lives of the Maya of Indiantown to wider networks of Maya and non-Maya people and institutions.

FOUR

THE MAYA IN COMMUNITY AND ETHNIC CONTEXT

Once in the United States, the Maya encounter a society centered on jobs and work. A person's identity is defined by work; social relationships are drawn along work and class lines; work itself or the lack of it is laden with value. Work has a strong position in the Maya system of norms as well. As Elmendorf (1976) points out, for the Yucatec Maya, work is highly valued in indigenous Maya communities. The Maya term for "friend," for example, literally mean "someone who works alongside you." It is a compliment to both Maya women and men to say that they are "real workers." And as Manning Nash (1967) shows in his classic study of a highland community undergoing change, the ethic of hard work among the Maya is one of the reasons why the cultural changes due to the introduction of a factory are relatively few. But while wages are important for the Maya, they do not overwhelm domestic and social relationships as they do in the United States.

To the diverse multiethnic population of Kanjobal Maya refugees, Mexican and Central American immigrants, and Haitians in Indiantown, labor and immigration policy is not an abstract legal concept but an everyday experience. The legal status of the work force of the area is in flux. Many workers have received permanent or temporary resident alien status under the provisions of the 1986 Immigration Reform and Control Act, others are awaiting the results of political asylum applications, and still others are recent and undocumented arrivals. These people live and work alongside African Americans and whites and articulate with the larger social and economic region of South Florida.

Indiantown had an official population of 4,794 according to the 1990 census, and the population projections based on the Martin County Comprehensive Plan (1985, 1987) for the Indiantown area anticipated that the permanent resident population would double through the decade of the 1990s. That number nearly doubles during the peak migrant labor season of October through May. Temporary workers are needed in the citrus fields each year, and the availability of alternative work in other labor markets such as construction draws an increasing number of immigrant workers, both documented and undocumented.

This chapter uses the community as the locus of inquiry to show how the labor market, the agricultural and nonagricultural industries, ethnicity, and immigration policy affect Maya migration to the town. In addition, the focus on the community of Indiantown illustrates how immigration and the strategies of informal and formal occupations mix together and influence change in areas such as gender roles, ethnic relations, and social services. The local labor force has changed rapidly during the last decade, a change that reflects the industry trends in the area, the arrival of new workers with different social and economic needs, and the course of civil strife in Central America. The community focus has the advantage over industry, labor sector, or ethnic group approaches, because it allows us to understand why different workers choose particular jobs in a context of multiple employment opportunities.

This chapter provides information on how immigrants to

Indiantown find work, how they use different labor markets, how their personal and cultural histories shape their work, and how these issues articulate with the social structure of the community. Much of the statistical data on the adaptation of the Maya and other groups to the community is based on a survey that was conducted in 1988 by anthropologists including Manuel Vargas, Joan Flocks, Julian Arturo, and Jerónimo Camposeco. Manuel and Joan are fluent in Spanish and Haitian Creole; Julian in Spanish and English, and Jerónimo in Maya, Spanish, and English. Seven questions were explored: (1) How does an immigrant's previous work affect his or her U.S. employment? (2) How does immigration status affect work prospects, job mobility, and job success? (3) How has the labor market in the United States affected male and female roles and expectations? (4) What are the relationships of different ethnic groups in the community in and out of work? (5) How has informal sector work supplemented formal sector work among these different groups? (6) How do immigrants find work and what is the role of public and private programs of work assistance and job referral? (7) What is the impact of the 1986 Immigration Reform and Control Act (IRCA) on these people in the community of Indiantown?

Named after an old Seminole Indian encampment, Indiantown was founded as a railroad stop at the turn of the century. Because it is close to Lake Okeechobee, Indiantown has historically served as a Florida sport base. A prominent hotel, the Seminole Inn, for example, was constructed in the 1920s as a genteel base for northern sportsmen and -women who visited this part of Florida to hunt and fish. Agriculture has also played an important part in Indiantown's history. Immense cattle ranches are still found to the north of the community, and the surrounding area is rich in citrus and winter vegetable fields. As one resident put it, "We're right on the line between the citrus and the winter vegetable farms. The citrus starts here and goes north; the vegetable farms are south of us." The community has over fifty thousand acres of citrus groves surrounding it, including some five thousand acres of lemon groves, possibly the highest concentration of lemon groves in the world.

Like many agriculture-dominated communities, Indiantown today is being encroached upon by commercial and residential development. A large Pratt and Whitney aircraft manufacturing plant built in the 1960s, twenty miles south of Indiantown, provides employment opportunities for over three thousand skilled workers in the aerospace industry. The labor force of the plant is made up of almost entirely local, nonimmigrant residents of the town and surrounding areas. In addition, new planned communities for retirees and others moving to Florida from other parts of the United States are creeping westward across the state toward the Indiantown region. Located in a high-growth region of Florida, on the fringes of the affluent retirement zone that stretches along the beaches from West Palm Beach to Jupiter, Indiantown provides an economical home site for less affluent retirees. The community boasts a retirement development of its own, Indianwood. A modest development of "manufactured housing," or permanent trailers, built on a golf course, Indianwood has added a new residential look to the total community.

Indiantown is not incorporated. Consequently, regular statistics on the population and other community characteristics are few. They include U.S. census figures and comprehensive plans for Martin County, which surrounds the community. Indiantown is at the extreme west end of the county, outside the population and growth centers of Stuart and Jupiter on the Atlantic coast. Most information about the area concerns what is referred to in civic and development circles as the "Treasure Coast," which includes Vero Beach, Fort Pierce, Port St. Lucie,

A Maya family poses in front of their rental home.
PHOTO BY MARIA ROCHA

During the festival of San Miguel, Maya from many other communities travel to Indiantown to see friends. Pedro Francisco and his wife, Juana, came to the festival from a migrant camp in South Florida.
PHOTO BY ALLAN BURNS

The three queens of the festival represent the community, workers, and sports teams. PHOTO BY ALLAN BURNS

Soccer matches, such as this one held during the festival, are an important link between the Maya communities of South Florida and other Hispanic communities. PHOTO BY ALLAN BURNS

Jerónimo Camposeco and Maria Rocha talk during a soccer match at the festival. PHOTO BY ALLAN BURNS

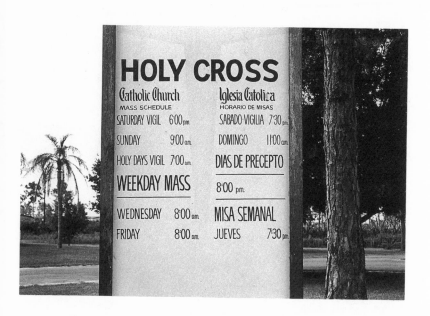

The Catholic church in Indiantown holds masses at different times for English- and Spanish-speaking parishioners.

PHOTO BY ALLAN BURNS

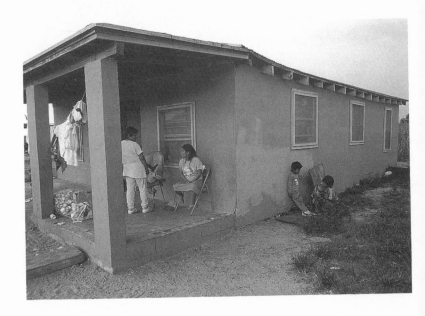

Several families share this migrant home.
PHOTO © ERIC BREITENBACH

Housing in Indiantown is in short supply and in poor condition.
PHOTO BY JOAN FLOCKS

Rental housing is scarce but preferred by the Maya.
PHOTO BY MARIA ROCHA

Donated clothing is sometimes dumped on a family's doorstep, where useful items are selected from the heap.

Field workers return home in the late afternoon.
PHOTO BY GREG MACDONALD

The Maya meet Mexican Americans and other Hispanics in the vegetable fields of South Florida. PHOTO © ERIC BREITENBACH

A clothing cooperative, InDios, was started by a group of Catholic nuns to provide steady work for migrant families.
PHOTO BY MARIA ROCHA

The population of Guatemalan Maya in Indiantown is increasing rapidly, as children are born one after another.
PHOTO BY JOAN FLOCKS

Family ceremonies such as weddings allow Maya to express their heritage through clothing, language, and activity.
PHOTO BY ALLAN BURNS

A small circus brings entertainment to Indiantown.
PHOTO BY MARIA ROCHA

Playing the marimba provides both prestige and a social context for friendship. PHOTO BY ALLAN BURNS

In Indiantown, Maya encounter people of other ethnic backgrounds.
PHOTO BY JOAN FLOCKS

Stuart, West Palm Beach, and Boca Raton. These are affluent areas that live up to the general image of South Florida promulgated by their chambers of commerce: beaches, golf courses, condominiums, and planned retirement communities. These areas are important in the context of immigration and ethnicity because they are the regions of construction work, service occupations (hotel work, etc.), and other industries that draw workers from the seasonal agricultural labor around Indiantown.

Indiantown's geographic profile reflects its origin as a railroad stop, so that from the beginning it was an open community (Wolf 1957). The community consists of several different neighborhoods or areas surrounded by citrus fields spreading along state highway 710, which has taken the place of the railroad as the major transportation avenue of the community. The community is made up of three general areas: Indiantown proper, Booker Park, and the Indianwood retirement development.

Indiantown proper consists of a series of commercial establishments lining the highway, centered at the community's only stop light. A large grocery store, several convenience stores, a post office, the public schools, and many smaller establishments mark this commercial center of the community. Surrounding this center are the houses of long-term residents, most of whom are white U.S. citizens. This area, known as "uptown," is a preferred place to live, and Mexican and other Hispanic residents move there when their economic status improves.

A mile to the north of the uptown area is an extensive neighborhood known as Booker Park. Booker Park has been the traditional residential area for agricultural workers. Today it consists of several apartment complexes known as "camps" where Kanjobal workers live, several streets of dilapidated houses where American blacks, Haitians, and other Hispanics live, and a federally funded housing project, New Hope, where legal resident agricultural workers can live. In Booker Park, 90 percent of the houses and apartments are rented. The area is notorious for the condition of its housing: open sewers abound, houses that are little more than wooden shacks are the norm, litter and health dangers are pervasive. For example, although only 7 percent of the Martin County population lives in Indiantown, all of the known cases of Trichuris, Shigella, and tapeworm have occurred there, most of them in Booker Park.

Over the years many attempts to improve the physical setting of the neighborhood have been made, such as the creation of the agricultural worker housing of New Hope. Still, residents are quick to note the housing problems in Booker Park. One young black woman related her shock at encountering the poverty of the area even when compared to her native New York:

> When I first came down here I said, "My God, if this were New York, they would tear these houses down." They wouldn't let people live in something like that. You know when you watch those movies about kids in Ethiopia? Those shacks they live in? That's how I saw it when I first came down here. My sister showed me her house and I said, "Yeah, right. Where do you live at? This must be your storage room or something." She said, "No, this is where I live at," and I couldn't believe it. (Flocks, fieldnotes, 1988)

When people can, they move out of Booker Park, as did the resident discussed above. New immigrants, including the Maya refugees from Guatemala, take their place. The house described above is now the home of a Maya family. The earlier resident's sister describes it today:

> That house is still the same. My sister lived there from eighty-three to eighty-five with no windows. Every year, we'd put plastic up to the window so the kids wouldn't

catch pneumonia. It was disgusting. The sewer hole that
was in the backyard—you're supposed to drain them?—[the
landlord] would never drain them and when someone used
the bathroom it'd come up through the kitchen sink. The
floors were caved in and the ceiling had big holes and then
they had that tin roof, half the wood was worn off. She had
rats in her house as big as my glass here. And the landlords,
they don't do anything. They don't do nothing at all for
those people. (Flocks 1988:92)

The interplay of these three residential areas—Indiantown
proper, with its commercial and institutional structure; Booker
Park, with its infamous streets; and Indianwood, located half-
way between the two and made up of manufactured retirement
dwellings—reflects the history of making a living in the community. The nicer "uptown" area continues to be the residential area of the more affluent. These include citrus grove man-
agers, workers at the Pratt and Whitney plant, local business
employees, and social service employees. The area contains an
abandoned rodeo field, testament to the time during the 1940s
and 1950s when cattle ranching was the area's primary economic base.

Expansion of the vegetable farms in the 1940s brought the
need for agricultural workers. Booker Park was settled by these
workers, mostly African Americans who came from other parts
of Florida. Through the 1940s to the 1960s, African Americans
and Puerto Ricans were the mainstay of the South Florida agricultural laborers. Working conditions for these people were brutal. A federal class action discrimination suit, for example,
which remained unsettled for over twenty years, alleged that
women working as agricultural field laborers in the 1960s and
early 1970s were regularly raped by crew leaders. In 1988, a
number of black women still living in the area were offered a

$550,000 settlement by the largest citrus operation of the area, Caulkins Groves (Gainesville *Sun*, May 30, 1988).

The citrus industry experienced its expansion in the 1960s and 1970s; agricultural land in Martin County increased by some sixty thousand acres between 1978 and 1982, for example (Regional Comprehensive Plan, 1987). To meet the needs of this industry, Mexicans began arriving in the community, brought by crew bosses who were contracted by the growers to provide laborers. Mexican and Mexican-American citrus workers from the West found the Indiantown area and the citrus industry of Florida a rich area for work. Competition was less intense than in the Western groves, and because the industry was concentrated, travel to different groves was easy.

It was at the end of this expansion, between 1983 and 1984, that the first wave of Kanjobal Maya came to the community seeking refuge and survival. As with many migrations of this type, a few families arrived and found both social and economic opportunities in the area. Frank O'Loughlin, the Catholic pastor of the Indiantown community in the early 1980s, expressed his anger at the way the Kanjobal Maya have been recruited as they cross the border: "In general, when people come across the border, they run into the horrible labor recruitment system that the agricultural industry has. The crew boss types pick them up—they're like vultures ready to prey on the weakest ones. The Guatemalans are targets for them."

During this same time a number of Haitians came to Indiantown from other areas of Florida to work in the groves and fields. In 1979 there were only three Haitians living in the community; in 1985 the number had increased to ninety-five (Dorman 1986:15). Haitians are industrious and admired by other ethnic groups for their skills and hard work, but are often confused with American blacks because of racial stereotypes.

Within the different areas of Indiantown there are known

neighborhoods where each ethnic group lives. In our survey, for example, 76 percent of the Kanjobal Maya lived in three apartment camps; 53 percent of the Mexicans lived in one camp. Residential segregation by ethnicity in Indiantown occurs even though most neighborhoods are multiethnic. Apartment complexes such as Blue Camp are known as the homes of recent arrivals. In the past decade this has meant the Maya.

In short, the history of Indiantown is one of dramatic changes in the immigrant and agricultural worker population. These dramatic changes are indicative of immigration in general in the United States in the 1980s, and they serve to make immigration policy especially important to the quality of life in the United States.

Estimates of the migrant and immigrant population of the community from residents and social service agency workers range from three to four thousand during the harvest season of October through May. But an adequate census of the immigrant population of Indiantown is not possible. The immigrant population is very mobile; individuals with few possessions find it easy to move quickly to other locations. For example, Pablo Fernandez, a twenty-eight-year-old Kanjobal Maya, came to Indiantown in January, leaving his wife and two children in his home country. In Indiantown he lived in a camp with nine other compatriots. The camp was especially dangerous: interethnic murders, robberies, and fights were common. Consequently, in August Pedro and six other men moved to a single room in a slum of West Palm Beach. It took Pablo ten minutes to pack up, and he slept on the floor at a friend's house in Stuart for a week before finally moving to his new room in West Palm Beach.

Since the enactment of the immigration reform act in 1986 (IRCA), however, more immigrants have looked for ways to stay in the area rather than move up the migrant stream with the uncertainties, low wages, family stress, and physically demanding work that comprises life as a migrant worker. The farm-worker amnesty portion of IRCA has been especially important in Indiantown. This provision gives resident alien status to farmworkers who are not eligible under the provisions of the law that granted legal status for undocumented immigrants who came to the United States before 1982. An undocumented immigrant who came after 1982 and worked a total of ninety days in agricultural labor between 1985 and 1986 is eligible for the "farmworker amnesty" or SAW (seasonal agricultural worker) or, more recently the RAW (replenishment agricultural worker) provisions of the 1986 act. Although earlier waves of Mexican agricultural workers in Indiantown did indeed come prior to 1982, the majority of the present farmworker popula-tion has arrived since that date.

As many researchers have pointed out, the 1986 Immigration and Control Act is a complex, changing law that policymakers find as difficult to understand as immigrants do (North and Portz 1988). Dramatic changes make it difficult to understand the policy or gauge its effect. Changes in regulations, differing interpretations, and decisions by the judiciary have made its implementation difficult. The effects of this act, as well as of previous immigration policy, have been distributed differently within the various ethnic groups of Indiantown. Mexicans in Indiantown have been in the community longer and tend to have had more experience with immigration in general and with the requirements for documentation to prove their em-ployment in farm labor during the time that the farm work amnesty provision of the law was in effect. The Maya have continued to come to the community at a regular rate. Those who have arrived after 1986, when provisions for legal residency could not be obtained under the law, have used political asylum as a strategy to obtain working papers for the temporary period of one year. Using political asylum to obtain work authorization papers is complicated by the existence of a large number of asylum applicants from the early 1980s whose cases were extremely sound, being based on the violence that was consuming much of the northwestern highlands of Guatemala at that time. More recent asylum seekers, who tend to have less sound cases, have switched from applying through recognized legal assistance programs to using notary publics in Miami who fill out asylum papers for whatever price they can get.

The interplay among the options of applying for residency under the provisions of the 1986 IRCA law, seeking political asylum, remaining undocumented, and seeking illegal documentation made social service work in the Indiantown area very difficult. The one center funded by the Catholic church that handled most of the applications for the IRCA was overwhelmed during the height of the application period. Workers there, both voluntary and paid, generally worked twelve to fifteen hours a day, were unable to carry out very many of their other social service activities (emergency relief, health referral, community organizing), and suffered a high degree of emotional stress and burnout. One effect of immigration policy has been the change in this center to much more limited activity. Originally the center was a multipurpose agency, making important contributions to employment referral, community cohesion, political asylum, immigration, and other areas. Then, for two years, it was reduced to being an IRCA processing service. Now that the IRCA period for application is over, the center has changed its mission in the community, cut back on many services, and reduced the size of its staff.

Given the chance to attain resident alien status, all who can qualify do so. Once someone has proper work authorization, the choice is usually made to stay and work in the area rather than face the uncertainties of further migration. During the Southeastern drought of 1986, for example, migrants found very little work in other areas of the Eastern seaboard. Health workers reported that, after three or four months of seeking work as migrant laborers in the drought-stricken agriculture areas of the Southeast, the workers returning to Indiantown had lost considerable weight and were in worse health than when they left. Frank O'Loughlin describes migrant work for the Kanjobal:

FRANK O'LOUGHLIN: The Guatemalans don't have the physique, you know, for working in the oranges, to go up twenty-foot ladders with ninety-five pounds of oranges, so they tend to work more in the vegetables. We encourage that too, because we encourage people to stay here. We were worried that we wouldn't be able to protect somebody picked up by the border patrol up the road in the migrant stream in the summer, so we asked people to stay here during the summer even though you can starve here during the summer and uh . . . with the promise that we would help them out. The only pickin' here in the summer is in lemons. And the pay in lemons, we've documented that the pay in lemons has been ten to fifteen dollars a tub.

ALLAN BURNS: How long does it take to fill up a tub?

FRANK O'LOUGHLIN: We've documented that it sometimes takes two days to fill up a tub because . . . because, typically what happens is that you would get on a bus and go out to the gardens and then sit on the bus waiting for the fruit to dry off because it blemishes if it's handled while it's still wet. A lot of these go to the stores so they're not allowed to touch the fruit while it's still wet. When they get into it, it's very often during the summer rains, so there was a labor department investigation of the wage per hour and they showed that people actually do earn only fifteen bucks for two days' work.

Ethnicity in Indiantown involves country of origin, race, and language. Although outsiders, including some employers, lump all Latin Americans together, a major division in the community exists between the Kanjobal Maya people and Mexican and Mexican-American people. The Kanjobal Maya population is physically smaller, speaks a Maya language first and Spanish only second, and considers itself culturally distinct from the "ladino" or non-Indian population of Central America and Mexico. In Indiantown, the Maya are the newest group and often the one mostly discriminated against by all other ethnic groups. Mexican and Mexican-American workers in the community refer to the Maya as *indios* (Indians), a term of deprecation in Mexico. One Mexican agricultural laborer took one of the research team aside and said, as if confiding something of surprising importance, "You know, the Guatemalans are really *inditos* [little Indians]!" Like Mariel Cubans and Haitians in Miami (Portes and Stepick 1980), they are in many senses an unwanted immigrant group not only to the Anglos of Indiantown but to other ethnic groups as well.

In addition to Mexicans and Mexican Americans, the few other Hispanics who live in Indiantown are from El Salvador and Puerto Rico. The Haitian population of Indiantown is relatively small, numbering less than one hundred during the peak months of the year and less than fifty during the summer months.

According to officials at the diocese of West Palm Beach, where SAW records were kept, approximately two hundred Kanjobal Maya applied for this status compared to one hundred Mexicans, five other Hispanics, and about thirty Haitians. This count of only four hundred individuals is misleading in some respects, as it accounts for only those who applied for legal status under the SAW program and excludes those who gained residency status through political asylum, the 1982 residency requirement of IRCA, or the Cuban/Haitian entrant provision of the act. Still, the general proportion of the different ethnic groups as given in the SAW estimates reflect the immigrant population of Indiantown.

The following information on characteristics of the immigrant population is based on our sample and on ethnographic observations. In our survey of Indiantown, a sample of fifty-three Kanjobal Maya, twenty-four Mexicans, ten other Hispanics, and three Haitians was used to gather information. The proportion of respondents was specifically stratified in this way to reflect the general immigrant population that we were able to estimate through our own work and through estimates of health and social service workers in the area. Table 1 indicates the nationality and sex distribution of the sample.

The survey was carried out using the household as the unit of analysis with one person interviewed per household. Random sampling was not possible in the community. Instead, the ethnographic technique of sampling within housing areas was followed. A "snowball" procedure was used by which respondents suggested other households in their neighborhood to sample. Residents were interviewed until we had reached the proportional goal of each ethnic group.

The Indiantown immigrant population has many more males than females. Seventy-two percent of our sample respondents were male and 28 percent were female, a figure that compares with the estimate of a 70 percent male and 30 percent female application rate for SAW applicants in 1988 and a similar proportion described in a census of the Kanjobal in Indiantown conducted in 1986 (Miralles 1986). At first glance, these data conflict with the assertion made earlier that the Guatemalans arrived as family groups. However, many of these family groups were made up of a woman, a man, their children, and their

TABLE I
Ethnicity and Sex Characteristics

Group	Male		Female		Total Number
	Number	% of Total	Number	% of Total	
Maya	37	70	16	30	53
Mexican	18	75	6	25	24
Other Hispanics	8	80	2	20	10
Haitian	2	67	1	33	3

nieces and nephews. Now that some time has passed, the proportion of men in the community has become more apparent as these extended family members are now on their own.

There is a second reason why the disproportionate number of males to females should not be interpreted as evidence that immigrant laborers to Indiantown are only young, unaccompanied men. Most immigrants are either married or living in a conjugal union. Many of their wives, however, remain in their homelands. As circumstances and funds permit, spouses are brought into the country. Miguel Carlos worked here a year before returning to Guatemala to get his wife. Before she came, he described his work in the fields:

JERONIMO CAMPOSECO: What work do you do?
MIGUEL CARLOS: We're planting chili.
JERONIMO CAMPOSECO: Planting chili?
MIGUEL CARLOS: Yes.
JERONIMO CAMPOSECO: Do they pay you by the hour or by the day?
MIGUEL CARLOS: By the hour.
JERONIMO CAMPOSECO: How much do they pay you an hour?
MIGUEL CARLOS: $3.25.

JERONIMO CAMPOSECO: Are you working with other vegetables?

MIGUEL CARLOS: Yes. Squash, cherries, and tomatoes.

JERONIMO CAMPOSECO: Do you harvest oranges when they are in season?

MIGUEL CARLOS: No, because we can't reach the trees as easy as the Mexicans.

JERONIMO CAMPOSECO: And about how much do you earn a day in the fields?

MIGUEL CARLOS: As much as I work, because I'm paid by the hour.

JERONIMO CAMPOSECO: How many hours do you usually work?

MIGUEL CARLOS: Sometimes just four hours, five hours. When there isn't a lot of work, just three hours. Just enough to eat.

JERONIMO CAMPOSECO: To eat?

MIGUEL CARLOS: Just enough to eat. And also paying the rent, and the electricity.

JERONIMO CAMPOSECO: You have to pay for rent, the electricity, and food.

MIGUEL CARLOS: Yes, because here you have to bring your own food.

JERONIMO CAMPOSECO: If you have any extra, what do you do?

MIGUEL CARLOS: If there is any extra, I sent it to my wife in Guatemala.

JERONIMO CAMPOSECO: Do you think your wife is doing OK there in Guatemala?

MIGUEL CARLOS: Well, there isn't any work there at all, but she has a little cornfield.

JERONIMO CAMPOSECO: When you go to work, say on Monday, what time do you get up?

TABLE 2
Marital Status

Status	Number	% of Total
Married	51	57
Living with a partner	18	20
Widowed	1	1
Unmarried	20	22
Total	90	100

MIGUEL CARLOS: I get up at 4:00 A.M. to make my food for the day.

JERONIMO CAMPOSECO: You have to make your food for the day.

MIGUEL CARLOS: And then we go. We get to the fields at five or six.

JERONIMO CAMPOSECO: What kind of food do you eat?

MIGUEL CARLOS: Some little eggs, tomato.

JERONIMO CAMPOSECO: Do you make tortillas?

MIGUEL CARLOS: There is no time. We usually buy them in the store. Then we warm them up and carry them with us.

JERONIMO CAMPOSECO: You men make it because your wives aren't here?

MIGUEL CARLOS: Yes, I have to make the food. Some men have their wives here who help them with the food.

The labor force of new immigrants to Indiantown as reflected in this survey shows that some 80 percent are married, living with a partner, or widowed (Table 2). This fact suggests why so many of the new immigrants seek out jobs that are not migratory. Family responsibilities and the need for a stable environment for children are priorities for these new immigrants.

TABLE 3
Age Distribution of Respondents and Spouses

| | Respondent | | Spouse | |
Age	Number	% of Total	Number	% of Total
15–19	7	8	2	3
20–24	17	19	11	18
25–29	16	18	15	25
30–34	19	21	5	9
35–39	6	7	9	15
40–44	11	12	9	15
45–49	7	8	4	7
50–54	3	3	3	5
55–59	2	2	0	0
60+	2	2	2	3
Total	90	100	60	100

Mean age of respondents and spouses: 33.2
Note: Not all respondents claimed to have spouses.

The immigrant population is young, but contains a sizable group of people in their forties, as is seen in Table 3. There was no significant difference in the sample between the age distribution of either Maya or Mexicans and other Hispanics. The mean age of Mexicans, for example, was thirty-one and the mean age of the Kanjobal Maya was thirty. A Pearson's correlation between country of origin and age was only .189, indicating only a very slight correlation between the two characteristics. The Maya appear to be a much younger population on other grounds, however. As Miralles (1986) pointed out, Kanjobal families tend to have more and younger children than other migrant families in the area; as a result, they are a younger part of the migrant labor force when described as families and not individuals.

TABLE 4
Age Breakdown by Nationality

Age	Maya		Mexican		Other Hispanic		Haitian	
	Number	% of Total	Number	% of Total	Number	% of Total	Number	% of Total
15–19	7	13	0	0	0	0	0	0
20–24	9	17	7	29	1	10	0	0
25–29	9	17	3	13	2	20	2	67
30–34	13	24	2	8	3	30	1	33
35–39	3	6	3	13	0	0	0	0
40–44	4	8	7	29	0	0	0	0
45–49	5	9	1	4	1	10	0	0
50–54	3	6	0	0	0	0	0	0
55–59	0	0	1	4	1	10	0	0
60+	0	0	0	0	2	20	0	0
Total	53	100	24	100	10	100	3	100

Table 4 shows the ages of respondents of the sample by country of origin.

The immigrant labor force in Indiantown has generally been in the area for several years (Table 5). The mean year of arrival of our sample, for example, was 1982, although a sizable portion (17.7 percent) of the sample arrived between 1986 and 1988.

These data suggest that the immigrant population of Indiantown is divided between an older group and newer immigrants who have been in Indiantown less than four years. Ethnographic research indicates that the older group is made up of Mexican and Mexican-American families and the newer group is made up mostly of Guatemalan immigrants. The mix of Maya, Mexicans, other Hispanics, and Haitian immigrants reflects a change

TABLE 5
Year of Arrival in United States and in Indiantown

Year	Arrival in United States		Arrival in Indiantown	
	Number	% of Total	Number	% of Total
1948–1978	17	19	11	13
1979–1982	24	27	11	13
1983–1985	32	36	39	45
1986–1988	16	18	25	29
Total	89	100	86	100

Note: These data were unavailable for some of the 90 survey respondents.

in the ethnic makeup of communities like Indiantown. Although migrant and agricultural workers have usually been thought of as Mexican, Indiantown shows that immigration policy in the 1980s faces the challenge of new groups of immigrants with experiences different from those of Mexican migrant workers. Guatemalan immigrants, for example, are drawn to the Indiantown area not only because of work opportunities, but also because of the large community of other Kanjobal Maya living there. Indiantown is a place where they can live and raise their children and retain their language and community strength. Haitian immigrants, who first lived in large cities such as Miami, are now moving into rural communities. As North and Portz (1988) and others have pointed out, the IRCA has benefited Mexican rural laborers more than other groups with occupations other than agriculture.

In Indiantown the benefits of legalization were seen as so important that all ethnic groups who could qualify attempted to do so. Those who could not qualify sought other means of obtaining documents for work, such as submitting political asylum applications or procuring forged documents. Even without any documents, however, it was and still is possible to get work in the area.

Carlos Gaspar came from Mexico in mid-August of 1987. He had been in the United States several times before, but not within the time needed to receive work authorization papers. He came to Indiantown because his uncle had been there in the winter and had found work in construction. At 5:00 A.M. Carlos and his uncle drove out to a construction site where several acquaintances were working. The construction site was in an elegant development with golf courses and houses costing half a million dollars. There was a guard at the entrance to the development and another one at the entrance to the construction headquarters. His uncle went in to the employment office with him because Carlos did not speak any English. There the personnel director asked if Carlos had his papers. His uncle said yes, and the director gave them a work application form. But there was no work that day. The director told Carlos to come back next week when a new building would be started. Carlos had worked a variety of construction jobs in Mexico before he came to the United States. He had experience in the oil fields of Tabasco and the housing industry of the border cities. He was confident he would get work the next week. When he was asked about getting papers, he shrugged and said, "I'll take my chances and see what I can find." A month later Carlos came by with a healthy look and a smile on his face. "Did you find work?" I asked him. "Sure, in construction," he answered. I asked if he had gotten his work authorization papers. "Sure," he answered, although it was doubtful that he had received official ones.

This chapter describes how the Kanjobal and other Maya who have come to Florida articulate with the community and with other ethnic groups found there. Unlike communities of Maya people in Mexico or Guatemala, the Maya of the United

States have become members of multiethnic communities. Indiantown, Florida, is not a refugee camp or a farmworker camp. It is an example of a rural small town, similar to crossroads and agricultural communities throughout the United States. When the Maya arrive in places like Indiantown, they put themselves into an environment of social class, ethnic diversity, and institutional complexity that is quite different from that found in traditional Maya communities. Part of the culture shock they encounter is due to these new community structures.

FIVE

WORK AND CHANGES IN SOCIAL STRUCTURE

As poverty-stricken migrant workers, Maya and other immigrants to Indiantown find identity through work. Work, and the identity that it provides people in the United States, varies according to the seasons of agricultural produce, the success of the South Florida construction industry, and the availability of papers giving them authorization to work legally. Work in Indiantown includes traditional field work picking oranges and vegetables in South Florida's large agricultural industry, construction in the affluent areas of the east coast, golf course and landscape construction, and work in the area's service industries. In addition, informal sector employment, including babysitting and cooking for women and recycling and small-scale selling for both sexes, plays an important role in the survival of the Maya and other immigrants.

In addition, those who have access to transportation and are unencumbered by small children travel north each summer when the vegetable crops of South Florida have been harvested—"the North" being any state from Oregon to New York where there are summer vegetables and fruits to be picked. During this period, the Maya are dispersed into small groups of one or two families for several months. The festival of San Miguel, described in Chapter Three, corresponds to the time when

TABLE 6
Predominant Economic Activity in Country of Origin

Activity	Maya		Mexican		Other Hispanic		Haitian	
	Num-ber	% of Total	Num-ber	% of Total	Num-ber	% of Total	Num-ber	% of Total
Subsistence agriculture	30	72	13	57	3	30	1	50
Commerical agriculture	1	2	1	4	5	50	0	0
Agriculture and commerce	3	7	0	0	0	0	0	0
Agriculture and craftwork	7	17	1	4	0	0	0	0
Mining	0	0	1	4	0	0	0	0
Tourism/ public works	1	2	5	22	1	10	0	0
Factory work	0	0	2	9	1	10	1	50
Total	42	100	23	100	10	100	2	100

Note: These data were unavailable for some of the 90 survey respondents.

the Maya return from this summer migrant work in northern states.

As Table 6 points out, by far the most common occupation held by Indiantown immigrants prior to coming to the United States was some form of agricultural work. These figures closely resemble those for SAW (seasonal agricultural worker) applicants under the IRCA, according to agency workers in the area. Nine out of ten Haitian SAW applicants who applied for legal status in 1988, for example, had been subsistence agriculturalists in Haiti before coming to the United States.

Agricultural work in the country of origin, however, is quite different from such work in the United States. Agricultural labor in the United States is singular in its approach: workers do one thing, such as spray orange trees, pick peppers, or weed flower fields. A subsistence agriculturalist in Mexico or Guatemala, on the other hand, grows several crops in his own plot each year. For the most important of these—corn, beans, and other subsistence crops—success requires a profound knowledge of soil types, rainfall, and local varieties. In addition, some cash crops, such as coffee or tobacco, may also be grown. A subsistence agriculturalist also raises cattle and pigs, hunts, and arranges for credit. In addition he may be a member of a cooperative for selling excess produce and cash crops. As a cooperative member he has full voice in decisions about prices and markets. When he is not working the subsistence and cash crops of his own land, he may hire himself out for wage agriculture. If this is not available, he may be a member of a craft or artisanry cooperative along with his wife. There they both might weave blankets and other tourist items or make furniture for local consumption. In short, work in the United States represents a tremendous step down in terms of the control that agriculturalists have over their own activities, the decision-making power they hold, the complexity of the agricultural tasks they perform, and the interplay of agriculture with other pursuits.

Even if immigrants were something other than farmers, the difference between what they did in the sending country and what they do in a similar industry in the United States is striking. Someone who builds houses in Haiti, for example, is skilled in business, machinery repair, and a variety of other tasks. A housebuilder must sell his skill to a client, saw boards from logs by hand, make concrete blocks individually by casting them one at a time, complete the plumbing and electrical wiring, if used, and construct doors and windows for each dwelling.

Important activities for both men and women in other countries, such as selling items in an open market, simply do not exist in the United States. The closest institution of similar form is the flea market. Not all immigrant groups take advantage of these markets as work opportunities. While Mexican-American immigrants have moved into vending roles in South Florida flea markets, for example, Maya and Haitians tend to go to them as entertainment. Flea markets are dangerous for undocumented immigrants, however. While research was being carried out for this study, a large flea market was raided by the Immigration and Naturalization Service in an attempt to catch and deport undocumented workers and their families.

Agricultural labor within the unskilled categories of fruit and vegetable harvesting was the economic strategy followed by almost all Indiantown immigrants upon arrival. Table 7 illustrates this by comparing the first and most recent jobs in the United States for the sample of this study.

Mexicans and Maya tend to work in single occupations. Occupational mobility either within the same sector or to a similar sector such as nurseries or golf courses is the preferred strategy. A farm laborer learns to drive and buys a vehicle as quickly as possible, for example, in order to become a subcontractor of a crew boss and recruit day laborers for work in different orange or lemon growers. Cooking and baby-sitting are common informal work strategies among women, especially for women who are too ill to go to the fields or who have children too small to be left with others.

Haitians, by contrast, are much more likely than Hispanic immigrants to have multiple strategies, including more varied jobs, informal economic activities, and vocal demands for better wages and conditions. Haitians come to Indiantown and other South Florida communities with more diverse and more urban experience than Latin Americans. Many of them have moved to Indiantown from Miami in order to escape the crime

TABLE 7
First Job in United States versus
Current Job in United States

Employment	At Time of Arrival		Current	
	Number	%	Number	%
Fruit/vegetable harvester	37	52	28	35
Other agricultural laborer	12	17	5	6
Construction worker	8	11	7	9
Nursery and landscaping worker	3	4	4	5
Machine operator (tractor driver)	3	4	12	15
Janitor, cleaner	2	3	1	1
Golf course construction worker	1	1	10	13
Restaurant worker	1	1	3	4
Social worker or community organizer	0	0	2	2
Child care worker	0	0	2	2
Crew leader	0	0	2	2
Other	5	7	5	6
Total	72	100	81	100

Note: These data were unavailable for some of the 90 survey respondents.

and violence there. These prior experiences have preadapted the Haitians to more employment diversity than the Maya and Mexicans, whose experiences in other parts of the United States tend to be rural and farm-work related. Recycling, petty selling and barter, flea market vending, and hotel work are areas where Haitians have moved to diversify their employment strategies much more quickly than other groups. Drug dealing and relying on public assistance are also economic activities that some Haitians resort to, but they are not condoned by the community. It is common to see handwritten paper signs on doors and buildings in a neighborhood telling drug dealers to stay away. Haitians in Indiantown feel that they suffer greatly from the negative stereotypes that publicity about the drug trade has given them. They claim that drug dealing was something that was learned in the United States by earlier immigrants and that is now spreading to recent arrivals.

Work becomes more varied for immigrants in Indiantown over time. For several reasons, immigrants quickly abandon agricultural labor when they can. First of all, few recent immigrants enjoy agricultural labor as it is organized in the United States. Mexicans who have done migrant agriculture for many years are likely to stay with field work longer than Maya and Haitians. The Maya, although many have expert agricultural skills, find it difficult to match the speed of the physically larger Mexicans. The form of work in the fields—picking one crop from sunrise to sundown—is of course known in other countries. But there it is only one of the many parts of agricultural production. Here it is the only job. Manuel Ignacio describes the uncertain work in the orange groves:

ALLAN BURNS: How is this orange picking where they pay you per box?

MANUEL IGNACIO: Yes. They pay you for each box.

ALLAN BURNS: How much, ten dollars?

MANUEL IGNACIO: No. They pay very little. Six.

ALLAN BURNS: And how many boxes can you pick a day?

MANUEL IGNACIO: According to how you work. If you work real hard, you can get six or seven. Or even eight if the oranges are good. But if there aren't a lot on the tree, you can only pick four. But it's really hard work. It kills you. The oranges are real heavy. If the tree has a lot of oranges, you get excited about working. But if it doesn't, you kill yourself running up and down that ladder with the oranges. You tire yourself more and you don't make anything. In contrast, when the tree has lots of oranges, you don't get tired and you make a lot too! You don't have to run much and you don't have to move the ladder. But when there aren't oranges, you kill yourself moving it.

A second reason for not staying in agricultural field work is that the work demands mobility. Immigrants are, as we saw earlier, often married. Even though agricultural field work pays better than other occupations in the area, the costs of transportation, setting up new residences several times a year, and times without work make it a difficult economic strategy for family survival.

Finally, agricultural work is dangerous. Pesticides, accidents in the fields or in transit, and robberies and muggings are all reasons for moving out of field labor as quickly as possible. Each year in Florida, farmworkers are poisoned when they go out into the fields too soon after the fields have been sprayed with poisons. Women and men who work in the fields around Indiantown as new immigrants are especially susceptible to developing skin rashes and other maladies from the heavy use of chemical pesticides and fertilizers, which adhere to the crops. Maya women were surprised at the number of skin ailments they had in the first few years of their lives in Florida. Because they are unfamiliar with the use of many of the chemicals common to U.S. agriculture, they seldom take proper precautions by wearing protective clothing, washing themselves and their clothing upon returning from the fields, and keeping out of the way of crop-dusting planes and helicopters.

As Table 7 shows, some work similar to agricultural labor attracts immigrants after they have been in the area for a period. Golf course construction and maintenance and nursery work are jobs that immigrants move on to quickly if given the chance.

Maya often find work in South Florida's burgeoning golf course construction industry. Many golf course grounds keepers and construction bosses say that Guatemalans are their first choice as workers. The reasons for this are complex. For one thing, more Maya were subsistence, as opposed to commercial, agriculturalists in their homeland than other groups. Subsistence agriculture demands a careful husbandry of plants. Golf course construction, with the need for extreme care in planting and caring for the different kinds of grasses, is analogous in that personal attention yields clear benefits. A second reason why the Maya find work in the golf course construction industry is that they are docile workers. Few speak any English at all, and so they work hard all day doing the tedious work of the industry without complaint, a trait highly valued by employers. Although tedious, the work is at least steady and less seasonal than agricultural field work. It allows them to stay in the area with their friends and families. Carlos Cuxim describes his golf course work:

> JULIAN ARTURO: Now that you are going to get your residency card, are you going to change your occupation or do the same thing?
>
> CARLOS CUXIM: I don't know what I will do yet. Things are better now here with the permission. I can work anywhere at any kind of job now. I am working in golf construction now.
>
> JULIAN ARTURO: In what?
>
> CARLOS CUXIM: In golf course construction. I'm working now putting in pipes for—how do you call it?—"irr . . ." where you put pipes in "ingre . . . irrigation"; how do you call it?
>
> JULIAN ARTURO: Yes, irrigation for watering.

CARLOS CUXIM: I'm working with that. Putting in four-, five-, six-inch pipes in the ground.

JULIAN ARTURO: Is that better than picking fruit?

CARLOS CUXIM: Oh yes. I hardly work in the fields any more. There's more work in the golf course. I started here, then I went to work in Palm Beach Gardens, and now I'm back here. After you get a little experience in golf construction, you can work at others.

JULIAN ARTURO: Do they pay better than in the fields?

CARLOS CUXIM: Yes, they pay a little bit better and they don't order us around as much. In contrast, in the tomato fields where you pick tomatoes, they . . . they order us around a lot. We're contracted and so they order us around a lot. On the other hand, in these golf construction jobs they treat you better. You have rights.

JULIAN ARTURO: Are there other people like Mexicans working there too?

CARLOS CUXIM: Yeah, there's Mexicans, other Guatemalans. Once you have your work permit, you can work there. Without it, it's really difficult to find work.

JULIAN ARTURO: How much are they paying?

CARLOS CUXIM: They're paying five an hour; sometimes you can work up to ten hours. But more than anything, they treat us well . . . they treat us well.

Work in Indiantown is segregated by ethnicity and language. Not only does ethnicity play a part in the procurement of work; it affects job and economic mobility. As in golf course construction, the Maya, new to United States work patterns, are often preferred laborers for low-skill work. Their lack of English- and Spanish-language skills inhibits their protests over work that is dangerous, dreary, or physically demanding.

TABLE 8
Literacy among Respondents and Spouses in
a Maya language, Spanish, or English

Literacy	Number	% of Total
Read and write	95	60.5
Read only	11	7.0
Neither read nor write	51	32.5
Total	157	100.0

As Table 8 shows, the literacy rate is relatively high, certainly much higher than is commonly thought, if literacy in the Spanish and Maya languages is taken into account (see Table 9). This finding suggests that the image that policymakers and others have of these new immigrants as uneducated and illiterate is wrong. Literacy programs should take into account the impressive literacy rate in immigrants' first languages.

But being literate in one's native language does not necessarily mean one is literate in English. Of course, English language skills are very low among the immigrants. Less than a fifth of the new immigrants in this sample could understand or speak English. Of the sample, nineteen respondents, or 21 percent, were able to understand English; sixteen, or 18 percent, could speak it; and only ten, or 11 percent, could write in English. Their inability to understand, speak, or write in English leaves them susceptible to exploitation in many institutional settings, including, of course, work. Unlike the situation in Los Angeles that Peñalosa (1988) reported, however, Maya people in Indiantown are not learning Spanish at a greater rate than English. Indiantown, and the South Florida milieu within which the Maya live, presents English as the second most useful language after Maya.

TABLE 9
Primary Language Spoken by Respondents

Language	Number	% of Total
Kanjobal Maya	43	48
Jacaltec Maya	8	9
Spanish	31	34
Haitian Creole	3	3
Other, including English	5	6
Total	90	100

The relatively high rate of literacy in some language, 61 percent for all respondents, in comparison to the relatively low literacy in English, only 10 percent, is an important feature of this labor force. Only 32 percent of the sample had never been to school; 41 percent had been to school past the fifth grade. Literacy and the education skills needed to achieve it are not so much lacking as lost when immigrants reach Indiantown and find no context in which to expand on their knowledge. The low-skill agricultural and construction work that the immigrants do does not require literacy skills, and the long, tiring working conditions leave little time or energy to transfer literacy skills from their own language to English. English classes for immigrants have not been successful. Church and other volunteer services have provided classes in English as a second language, but attendance has been low because of exhaustion from working in the fields all day and the lack of regular classes appropriate to the needs of the different ethnic groups in the community.

The high rate of literacy suggests why it is that immigrants leave agriculture as quickly as they do. Literacy and education in their own cultural context make unskilled agricultural labor a kind of underemployment. Skills acquired prior to coming to the United States are not needed in the South Florida labor market, whether these skills are those used in technical areas such as agriculture or those gained in moving through the educational system into professional work.

Martin Demetrio had been in college in Guatemala prior to coming to the United States. He had worked in an agricultural extension station before the years of violence left him without a job and fearing for his life. He came to the United States and found a job making coffins in Pennsylvania. After a few years he moved his family to Indiantown to be near other Maya. He worked for a time for a church, became unemployed, and turned to contracting laborers for a citrus company because of his skills in English and his literacy. Like his friend Gaspar Domingo, Martin ruefully notes that his years of education and professional training are not usable here.

Gaspar Domingo had been a health promoter in Guatemala. He had university training in rural health delivery and was also employed as a radio announcer in the district capital. He has immigrated to Indiantown twice, once on his own and then again with his wife and children. Because his skills are desperately needed in the U.S. Maya community, he attempted to receive a working visa to come to the United States at the embassy in Guatemala City, but the application was turned down. He, his wife, and his two young children came anyway. One day he met an upper-class Guatemalan doctor in Miami. The doctor asked him, "Didn't you used to be at the San Felipe Hospital [a pseudonym]?" "Yes," Gaspar replied, "but now I'm here." "What are you doing here?" asked the physician. "Here I'm a tomato picker," answered Gaspar. The ironic and self-deprecating manner in which he replied indicated his frustration with his underemployment.

Since the passage of the 1986 Immigration Reform and Control Act, immigrants in Indiantown have been quick to apply for legal status. The act provided for Haitians whose arrival had been recorded by the INS before January 1, 1982, to receive permanent residency. In addition, Haitians also had the opportunity to apply under the principal program of legalization, one of the two seasonal agricultural worker programs, or other provisions of the act. Some were too wary of the INS to apply for any of these. Furthermore, like their counterparts from Guatemala, Mexico, and other Hispanic countries, those who arrived after 1986 did not have recourse to either temporary or permanent resident status. The Maya, as described in Chapter Four, had an additional strategy of using political asylum applications as a means for obtaining a temporary resident alien document for twelve months. The well-documented and publicized cases of political asylum application by Guatemalan refugees made this strategy viable, at least for obtaining documentation for a one-year stay in the United States. Mexicans and other Hispanics were not as fortunate in terms of other strategies. But Mexican immigrants generally had been in the country longer and were more likely to be able to prove that they had been engaging in farm work during the "window of opportunity" period covered by the seasonal agricultural worker provision— the twelve-month period ending on May 1, 1986. Nonetheless, one crew leader who was found hiring undocumented workers for contracted work said that over 90 percent of the farmworkers were still illegal two years after IRCA went into effect.

Under the IRCA, after a year sanctions were to go into effect against employers who hired undocumented workers. Consequently, larger employers in the agricultural industry began hiring only workers who had applied for legal status. Undocumented immigrants turned to smaller agricultural firms or did day labor in agriculture working for contracted "crew bosses" who could pay cash for work done. Hired by different employers to recruit laborers for different agricultural jobs, crew bosses are often paid the wages of all of the workers and are expected to pay social security and unemployment benefits for each worker. In practice, crew leaders are notorious for paying workers in cash and pocketing the money designated for benefits.

Illegal aliens cannot complain about their exploitation at the hands of crew leaders or labor contractors without fear of losing their jobs or being turned over to the Immigration and Naturalization Service. Even immigrants with documentation do not have a voice in farm labor. In the sample used in this study, 25 percent noted that they were members of a "labor association." When asked what the organization was, however, only eight individuals, or 9 percent, named a union. The others listed organizations such as the Kanjobal Maya association, a marimba music group, and recreational soccer teams. Union organizing among the Guatemalan refugees who do agricultural work in South Florida has not been successful. This has been due to the workers' lack of experience with unions in the predominantly Maya highlands of Guatemala, the inability of agricultural union organizers to make inroads into many migrant labor communities, and language differences between organizers and the Maya.

The other alternative for those who do not qualify for legal status under the IRCA provisions is to work at construction jobs where day laborers are given seventy-two hours to apply for a work permit. This allows these industries to maintain a large labor pool of very transient workers. Many workers have, of course, developed strategies to maximize the employment opportunities within this structure. They move from job to job every seventy-two hours or give false names and social security numbers to gain subsequent seventy-two-hour periods of work.

To a U.S. citizen, such behavior seems hardly worth the effort. But for immigrants these opportunities are wonderful. A low wage in the United States (less than four dollars an hour in construction, for example) is considered a handsome sum compared to the wage structure the workers may have been used to in Guatemala or Mexico. They may be from countries like Haiti, El Salvador, or Guatemala, which have only a limited economy left, or from countries where the minimum wage is abysmally low, such as Mexico, where the minimum rural *weekly* wage in the summer of 1988 was the equivalent of a dollar and a half. In such cases, even seventy-two hours represents a job opportunity that cannot be overlooked. While legal status is certainly sought after by all who can possibly attain it, those who cannot are resigned to a short but comparatively productive stay in the United States. Indiantown is one of the communities where both immigrants and employers know that work with a quick turnaround is better than no work at all.

Benefits of legal status that immigrants mentioned include access to unemployment compensation and other forms of assistance when needed. Those who work solely in the citrus groves need unemployment compensation during the long months from May until October or November when there are no oranges or lemons to pick. Immigrants are quick to point out that they would much rather work. If jobs in landscaping or construction are available during the off-season, immigrants will work at those until the higher-paying picking jobs return during the season. Legal status also allows people to work in industries such as construction and service that do not demand moving each year from the community, or to get jobs where their previous skills can be put to good use. Women with legal status, for example, can become teachers' aides, day-care workers, health auxiliaries, and Head Start program teachers. For women who were students or teachers in their countries of origin, such opportunities represent a welcome return to areas of skill and professional satisfaction.

Women's roles in the immigrant community of Indiantown are very different from those in their countries of origin. The most dramatic changes are in the workplace and in the home. In countries of origin, women seldom engaged in wage labor within the formal agricultural sector. They earned wages by cooking for groups of workers, selling in the market, working in cooperatives, and engaging in other activities. But they did not go to the fields to work alongside the men, except in their family gardens and subsistence plots.

In the United States, citrus and vegetable harvesting employs both men and women, and immigrant women have to take such work when it is available in order to augment the family income. This larger economic role has not translated into a lessening of marital or family bonds among recent immigrants such as the Maya. Maya are not motivated by romantic love in seeking a spouse; family arrangements or economic security are more common reasons for marriage than affection. Because of this, Maya women in Indiantown state that they readily leave an abusive or otherwise unproductive husband, though no more often than in Guatemala. For example, Juana Estrella, the wife of a successful farm laborer who has bought a van to transport workers to the fields to gain extra money, is giving up her job as a day-care worker to return to field work, where she will be able to keep an eye on her husband. She is concerned that he is getting drunk too often and losing the profits he makes as a subcontractor to one of the larger crew bosses in the area.

Women's roles in the household have changed most dramatically among the Maya and Haitians, and less so among the Mexican immigrants. Guatemalan and Haitian women have had to add their wage labor work to their already existing domestic work in child raising, cooking, and home organization. Haitian women, as mentioned, have been much quicker than Mexican or Maya women to move into nonagricultural labor, especially in nearby factories, restaurants, hotels, and stores. Some travel several hours a day to Orlando to work in the tourist hotels of that vacation city.

The average Guatemalan household contains between nine and fourteen members, half of whom are boarders not related to the owner of the house or apartment. Women cook for the entire household and receive some compensation from non-relatives. In Guatemala, women who cooked for others in addition to their families did so for short periods of time during harvests or during periods of wage labor. In the United States, this work is done in addition to wage labor. Juana Estrella has twenty-two people living in her house, only eight of whom are members of her immediate family. The rest are men without families in Indiantown. Juana arises each day at 4:00 A.M. to begin cooking for the household, then goes to work as a day-care worker at 8:00 A.M. In the afternoon she prepares food for her family and the boarders. Juana and her husband are among the more successful immigrants, yet there is no end in sight to her tremendous burden of work.

Women's roles vis-à-vis their children have also changed in Indiantown. Children from all the groups in the community are rapidly learning English through the public school and the church-supported migrant school. They become translators for their parents during visits to clinics, service centers, and stores. While at first glance this appears to be an example of successful language shift, it also places parents, especially mothers, in an unusual position. They are no longer the experts in the very areas in which they were highly skilled in their countries of origin: food, health, and security. Health care is an especially sensitive area. Local health care workers look to children as translators, but the extreme formality of many Hispanic women regarding subjects such as reproduction and bodily health make it difficult for them to use their children for this purpose. Children pushed to translate terms for bodily organs or processes often find that they do not know the terminology in the home language, and put their mothers in positions of embarrassment and discomfort.

Each ethnic group in Indiantown maintains considerable endogamy. Marriage partners seldom come from different ethnic groups. Immigrants can count on one hand the number of Mexicans who have married Maya people, for example. According to discussions with both men and women in the Guatemalan community, it is much more common for Guatemalan and Mexican men to have Anglo girlfriends or wives than it is for them to find partners in other Hispanic ethnic groups. Kanjobal women marry only Kanjobal men, and Mexican women almost always marry Mexican men. Haitian women seldom marry other than Haitian men, although because they have found more varied work in the larger society than have the other groups, they have to some extent been assimilated into the African-American community through marriage.

Interethnic relations in the community are not especially improved through work. Work is often thought of as the place where the "melting pot" ideal of U.S. society operates best. The common experience of labor, the structure of industrial relations, and the camaraderie developed on the job are all important ideas of how work contexts can function to assimilate people of different backgrounds. But in Indiantown, there is a strong motivation to seek work and other help from people who speak the same language in the community (see Table 10). Only occasionally is cross-language communication necessary.

Cross-ethnic group communication events seldom develop into friendship. The extreme physical demands of the jobs that immigrants hold preclude much talk. For example, one Haitian man recounted that a Mexican was hired to work on his crew in a landscaping business. The Haitian was a supervisor of the

TABLE 10
Resources for Finding Work

Strategy	Actual		Preferred	
	Number	% of Total	Number	% of Total
Friends	24	30	19	26
Family	12	15	13	18
Same ethnic group	13	16	6	8
Crew leader	4	5	0	0
"Blue Camp" apartment	3	4	3	4
Private labor center	19	24	5	7
Church service	4	5	4	6
Searching	1	1	17	24
Compadre (co-godparent)	0	0	1	1
Waiting	0	0	4	6
Total	80	100	72	100

Note: These data were unavailable for some of the 90 survey respondents.

Mexican and tried to learn several phrases in Spanish related to the work. After a few weeks however, he stopped trying. When asked if he had formed a friendship with him, he said he had not, because there was so little time to talk while working. Even times like lunch breaks were not used for socialization, because, as he noted, "it is a time for eating, not for talking."

Another Haitian had been given responsibility for driving a tractor. The tractor got stuck in the mud, so he asked an English-speaking friend how to explain his predicament to his boss. He was taught to say, "Boss, the tractor got stuck in the mud." He repeated the phrase often and wrote it down to memorize it. The next day he told his boss what had happened and resolved the problem. A few weeks later he was asked if he remembered the phrase, but he did not.

There are a few community contexts where interethnic relationships develop. The Catholic church, for example, offers masses in Spanish several times a week when all Catholic Hispanics meet together. Likewise some Baptist and other Protestant churches in the area hold services in Spanish. The ethnic groups are not monolithic in their loyalty to each other, either. Political divisions among the Maya, for example, include differences between those who supported the guerrilla uprising in the early 1980s and those who supported the military. Religious differences are very strong within the groups, and regional differences within the countries of origin are also expressed in Indiantown. These intragroup conflicts allow for interethnic relationships to develop, but in fact very few go beyond a relationship of joking acquaintance.

As we saw in Chapter Four, work referral was originally carried out by social workers at the Catholic church center in the course of assisting immigrants in seeking legal status. The void left when the center shifted its focus to other activities has been filled by two private work centers, located in Stuart and Jupiter, that are owned by a construction contractor who supplies labor to the growing industry of the Florida coast. The labor center provides buses to pick up workers in Indiantown and connects them with employers who have unskilled or semiskilled work. Up to seventy people a day take the labor center bus on the half-hour drive to the coast in the hope of securing work in the construction industry. Unskilled construction work drew a wage of four dollars an hour in the late 1980s and skilled work (carpentry, etc.) drew five dollars an hour. Since the labor center's service charges, as well as social security and other benefit charges, are deducted from this wage, however, a five-dollar-an-hour wage ends up netting under four dollars.

The complex cultures and experiences of the different immigrant groups in Indiantown have resulted in a layering of work by ethnicity as well as the development of different strategies of securing work authorization and resident alien documents. More importantly, ethnicity in communities like Indiantown influences the way workers organize themselves to do work. Those without English-language skills and those unfamiliar with U.S. work expectations are left with physically demanding jobs in the agricultural or construction industries. The uncertainty of their legal status, whether as applicants under the IRCA, as asylum applicants, or as seventy-two-hour day laborers, prevents them from protesting work conditions or terms of employment. Others, such as Mexican immigrants, who are more familiar with U.S. work patterns and have a longer cultural history of migration for employment, have an easier time securing legalization documents and so feel more confident about pacing themselves when they work in physically demanding contexts such as citrus or vegetable picking. They do not fear for their jobs in the fields because they are aware that growers greatly depend on their labor for the short harvest season. They live in smaller households than Guatemalans, and so women's roles are not radically different from those in Mexico.

Immigration policymakers have recognized that there are different expectations and perspectives among those affected by changes in laws or procedures. Generally the competing interest groups of politicians, government bureaucrats, the labor industry, national workers, and foreign nationals are recognized in policy formation and review. The Indiantown experience suggests that the cultural forces of ethnicity, the meanings of work and wages in different countries, and community social organization also contribute to the effectiveness of policy or its ineffectiveness.

The case of Indiantown illustrates that immigration policy is not easily implemented, even in relatively small labor markets such as this community of six to seven thousand inhabitants. Recent and historic immigration to the community has resulted in a complex configuration of resident and new workers. New workers from the Caribbean and Central America do not compete with local workers because the labor market is sectored by ethnicity and race. Haitian and American black men compete for some jobs, but the number of Haitians in Indiantown is very small, so this competition has not led to conflict. As difficult as it is, finding a job in Indiantown is not as difficult as finding a place to live, finding something to do when one is not working, or finding companionship. The availability of different kinds of work has drawn more new immigrants to the community, but their presence taxes the meager services that the community can provide. Overcrowding, family violence, public drunkenness, and a small town full of people who are strangers has brought Indiantown to a crisis. Older, mostly Anglo residents are quick to point out faults with the new immigrants:

"Just shoot them all. I wish I had a gun. I'd take care of them," said an elderly cowboy standing behind the supermarket in Indiantown one day.

"Why?" I asked incredulously.

"Look at them leaving their garbage from their lunches on my lawn!" he said. His anger was real. The Indiantown he had known as a cattleman was gone. In its place was a town full of unknown workers speaking strange languages.

SIX

CONFLICT AND THE EVOLUTION OF A NEW MAYA IDENTITY

Interest in ethnic identity in anthropology and the social sciences in general has increased dramatically in the past few years. The rise of ethnic politics and nationalism (Anderson 1983), the international indigenist movements of the 1980s and 1990s (Royce 1982), and the collapse of the Soviet Union in 1991 have all pointed to the importance of ethnic identity for understanding contemporary culture change among people like the Maya. While ethnic relations have always been an integral part of Maya society in Guatemala (see for example Nash 1989, De la Fuente 1967, Hawkins 1984, and Smith 1990), the experience of becoming exiles has resulted in the development of a different identity in the United States. The identity of the Maya of Indiantown is expressed through language, bulletins, social relations, festivals, and political organizations. The single experience of leaving Guatemala is one that has united Maya people. Added to this are the experiences of violence, the breakdown of the Guatemalan economy in the 1980s, and the reaction of North Americans toward the Maya. Even though not every Maya suffered the kind of violence that forced the early immigrants to Indiantown, the memory of the journey across Mexico into the United States is shared by all. In this chapter the evolving identity of the Maya in Indiantown is explored, especially as it is seen from both within and without the refugee community. Residence, work, leadership, religion, and communication are examined in this chapter to illustrate how this identity has changed through the Maya experience in Florida.

Identity has changed for the Kanjobal and other Maya in Indiantown as they have sought refuge in this multiethnic town. The new identity that is emerging is tempered through interethnic communication and conflict within the community. In addition, Maya external identity has evolved in the view of others in the community. The early image of the Maya, as presented in newspapers and local discussion, was one of sad and unusual victims of a war who faced great culture shock in the United States. Recently that image has shifted to one of the Maya refugees as migrant workers with little to offer the community aside from their work. These changes in identity occur in a context of shifting political structures and ethnic politics both here and in Central America.

In the United States, public interest in Central America declined in the 1990s as the Mideast and Europe began to dominate the media. Guatemalans and Central Americans in the United States were not as newsworthy by the 1990s as they had been in the 1980s, even though a second civil president was elected in Guatemala in 1990 and even though assassinations, the murder of villagers, and human rights abuses continued at an alarming rate in the early 1990s. From January through September 1991, for example, there were 638 reported assassinations and 1,718 cases of human rights violations, according to the Guatemalan Commission on Human Rights (*Times of the Americans*, October 4, 1991). The 1990 killing of Guatemalan anthropologist Myrna Mack and the subsequent murder of the chief investigator of her case brought some renewed attention to Guatemala in the U.S. media, but in general, focus on Guatemala declined.

Indigenous political movements increased in intensity worldwide through the beginning of the 1990s, giving the Maya of Indiantown a context within which they could begin to invoke their identity as a refugee indigenous group. Guatemalan Maya were active in indigenous human rights conferences in Geneva in 1984 and in Managua, Nicaragua, in 1986 (Arias 1990). Guatemala itself was the site for a major meeting of North and South American indigenous political activists in the fall of 1991. While the Maya of Indiantown did not send representatives to the conference, the international indigenous movements were well known to many people in the community. This, coupled with the breakdown of the Soviet domination over small countries in Eastern Europe, provided the language and framework for expressing a new Maya ethnicity in the United States.

The personal and group identity of refugees now in the United States who have fled Guatemala is an important issue for their own survival. Guatemalan Maya refugees have a very practical need for an identity apart from other undocumented aliens so that deportation can be forestalled when the Maya are brought before immigration officials. One issue of identity is their right to speak their own language. As Maya speakers, they must be provided with an interpreter during deportation hearings, for example. At a cultural level, the identity of the Maya refugees is important as a base for self-confidence and success as they face the rigors of living in a radically different environment. For example, since political asylum, while popular among civil liberties lawyers at the local level, has not been a viable means of maintaining legal status in the United States, the Maya have had to learn to adapt to the Immigration Reform and Control Act of 1986, discussed in Chapters Four and Five.

Maya identity in Indiantown is constantly renewed by common experiences in the United States and by recollections and conversations about Guatemala. In October 1991, for example, a car containing seven Guatemalans crashed in an irrigation canal in Indiantown. All occupants were killed. In a *New York Times* story on the crash, Antonio Silvestre remarks, "We have lived through tragedy after tragedy. . . . The indigenous peoples of Guatemala have always been exploited, marginalized and killed, so something like this merely enhances a feeling of solidarity in suffering." In the same story, Carlos Lopez, a Maya high school student, was interviewed about being Maya. He said, "I can still remember my grandma telling us that the soldiers were coming and that we would have to hide if we didn't want to be killed" (*New York Times,* October 24, 1991).

Both internal and external identity was first and foremost enhanced by the killings that the Maya witnessed in Guatemala. Pedro Antonio told me that he and his family left Guatemala when there was no place left to flee to:

> We were living in that town when my *compadre* [best friend] was killed. He and three others were killed one night. They shot him and left him on the street. We heard it. He was dying all night, and his wife was crying. No one could go out and help him because they were sure they would be killed. His wife was crying all night. The next morning we went out and he was dead. A bullet came in here [points to his stomach], and came out here [points to his back]; another one went in here [points to his head] and came out here [points to other side of head] and another one went in here [points to his forehead] and came out here

[points to back of his head]—*cruzado* [criss-crossed]! Well, later we went back to our own town; the same thing happened there! We had to leave because there was no where else to go, so we came here.

Indiantown is a small community where face-to-face contact and a legal assistance network that is effective in forestalling deportation make survival more feasible. Family connections and the vague hope of safe haven were important in people's decisions to come to Florida. One sixteen-year-old young man recalled his decision to come to Indiantown:

One morning I woke up and knew that I could not stay in Mexico by myself any longer. I knew there was a place in the United States called Indiantown, in a place called Florida, where an uncle and aunt of mine had gone when they escaped from Guatemala with their children. I did not know if they were still there, but since I could not go back to my home, I decided to go to Indiantown and try to find them. (Ashabranner and Conklin 1986:41)

Once in Indiantown, Maya refugees have had to adapt to a multiethnic migrant community. In addition, social workers and social service volunteers have become an important part of the social field of daily life in Indiantown. Church workers and volunteers, legal assistance lawyers and aides, hospital and clinic workers, as well as journalists, social scientists, and union organizers are now common actors in the social fields of the Maya.

A well-documented aspect of Maya cultural identity in Guatemala is the connection that people have to the communities where they were born (Nash 1989, Tax 1952, Wagley 1949). The coincidence of language, the town or community, and culture has been described as the basis for Guatemalan Maya identity.

Added to this local base is the long history of state intervention in local affairs in the process of identity formation in Guatemala (Smith 1990). The Maya of Indiantown certainly recall their home communities in Guatemala, but their identity today is informed by their experiences as immigrants in Indiantown. Some have passed through refugee camps in Mexico, others have lived in *barrios* in Los Angeles with other Maya, and others have lived as illegal aliens in the migrant streams of the United States. There are many more refugees in the refugee camps and cities in Mexico, for example, than in the United States. On one hand, this makes the relatively small number of Maya refugees in Indiantown seem less important than the total number of Maya refugees in the Americas. But Indiantown is connected to the experience of all Maya refugees, whether they are internally displaced people in Guatemala, in official camps in Mexico, or in cities in Mexico, the United States, or Canada. There is a flow of people through all these communities, so that experiences in one context become added to those of others. The identity of Maya in exile is one in which refugee locales like Indiantown are infused with a sense of belonging to a natal community in Guatemala. One Maya woman said that she did not feel that Indiantown was her home during her first few years of living there. "There are no graves of the dead here," she said. But within five years there were graves of Maya who had died in the United States, so Indiantown joined the home villages in Guatemala as a place where Maya identity is defined.

The evolving identity of the Maya in Indiantown can be seen in five areas where conflict and confrontation with people of other ethnic groups is present. These are residence, work, leadership, religion, and communication. Identity, as De Vos and Romanucci-Ros (1982:368) advanced the concept, indicates both a "shield" that protects people from outside threats and dangers and an "emblem" that provides self-awareness and confidence for individuals and groups. As a "shield," identity structures social relationships and can even, as Barth (1969) notes, provide a social field in which interaction can take place. The description of Maya identity in this chapter calls attention to the ways that the culture of the Maya persists in Indiantown. The concept of identity focuses attention on the ways in which the Maya have become a recognized group in the community, as well as on the ways in which the ethnic context of life in the United States has changed Maya ideas and activities, making their culture and social organization much different from that found in Guatemala.

Maya cultural identity is as much an internal feeling of belonging to a group of people (Anderson 1983) as it is an external set of perceptions and sometimes stereotypes that others have toward the Maya. This dual nature of identity as an external and internal entity is particularly important in the case of the Maya refugees, since they were a relatively unknown group in terms of their background, culture, and refugee status when they began to arrive in Indiantown. They have gone through changes in their external identity from welcomed strangers to tolerated farmworkers and disliked "invaders." Internally, they have changed from refugees shocked by their experiences to a diverse community of surviving Maya. As more and more people arrive in Indiantown from different Guatemalan Maya communities, a sense of pan-Mayanism is emerging. In an important sense, Indiantown is a place where Guatemalan Maya have become American Maya who take their place alongside other ethnic groups that are economically tied to the low-paying jobs in migrant agriculture and construction.

In the first few years of migration to Indiantown, residence was localized in a few camps like those described in earlier chapters. These buildings had rooms large enough to house more than one family. High rents (up to three hundred dollars a month for a two-bedroom unit) made sharing quarters with relatives, friends, and sometimes strangers a necessity. As more and more Maya refugees arrived, people took rooms wherever they could find them. This new kind of housing arrangement led to outbreaks of diseases such as tuberculosis and other social problems, but it also brought out the Maya sense of irony. Once a social worker asked a group of Maya what they had here that they did not have in Guatemala, expecting that they would mention things like fast food restaurants or better medical care. One young man, Pascual Martinez, answered sarcastically, "In Guatemala we do not have Blue Camp!" (the most dangerous of all the housing areas in Indiantown). He used this to construct his ironic humor about places of great personal danger in a land of safe haven.

Indiantown grew from a haven for a few Maya families in the early 1980s to a center of at least four thousand Maya by the end of the decade. But the lack of services and employment in the area led many Maya to move to small towns throughout the state. In the last half of the decade of the eighties, residence became dispersed throughout the region of South Florida, in a way replicating the dispersed *aldeas*, or hamlets, around a municipal center such as San Miguel in the highlands in Guatemala (Lovell 1988). Some families have struck out on their own to live with other migrant laborers, but many have moved to the small towns where friends and relatives from their natal villages in Guatemala live. Within South Florida, smaller Maya groups found in places like Lake Worth, Boynton Beach, Homestead, Immokalee, and West Palm Beach are known as communities of people from particular *aldeas* such as Coya or San Rafael. West Palm Beach has many residents from the municipal center of the Kanjobal area of Guatemala, San Miguel Acatán. Even within Indiantown, the lack of housing and the need for Maya people to take whatever housing is available has meant that they have ended up dispersed throughout the general community of the poor and migrant workers of the community.

For the Maya Indiantown functions as a center, even as a ceremonial center, important as a symbolic location as well as a place of residence. Their use of the community as an identifying locale is a residence pattern that the Maya people have retained from their past.

Crowded housing conditions with many unrelated people living in one apartment constitute an adaptation to the realities of poverty in the United States. Maya women report that they are learning to cook Mexican food, for example, as migrant workers from Mexico share houses with Maya families. As pointed out in Chapter Five, even the high number of people per household is an identifying characteristic of the Maya of Indiantown. Of course, most new immigrant groups use strategies of doubling up in houses or apartments to survive in countries with high costs, but the pattern in Indiantown is noticeably different from the housing patterns of other ethnic groups. In this local sense, then, crowded housing, especially in one of the "camps," is an identifying characteristic of the Maya.

The cultural use of space in the households in Indiantown is likewise a product of the Maya experience in the United States. Small areas are cordoned off with curtains for each family or boarder using part of the house, and the curtains are put aside during the day. Many women baby-sit, taking in children during the day, so the houses are full of young children for much of the daylight hours. Women share kitchen equipment to make food for those men and women who go to the fields as farm laborers. Handmade tortillas, beans, and occasionally chicken are prepared as farmworker food. Since many of the camp apartments have no refrigerators, food is kept on the stove all day.

Walls are left bare, except when a few *recuerdos,* or remembrances are available to hang on the walls: photographs of baptisms, marriages, and other events; souvenir weavings that say "Guatemala" on them; and perhaps a child's handwoven skirt or blouse. Windows are covered with curtains, often throughout the day, especially if there are young babies in the house, as mothers do not wish to expose them to outside dangers. In Guatemala, a darkened house made ecological sense in the cool and damp highland climate. In South Florida, darkened windows make another kind of sense: it is safer to have windows darkened because of the crime in migrant communities. A small black-and-white television is an early purchase, as is a VCR. During the day, televisions and rented movies create a background of noise, which also serves the important function of giving the impression that many people are in a house. The television and VCR are also important means of entertainment for Maya men and women who do not wish to go out at night and risk being attacked.

The Maya sense of identity as seen through residence is the result of poverty as well as cultural history. A person knows he or she is in a Maya household because of the aroma of the food, the crowded conditions, the darkness, and the children, as well as because of the people themselves and the language they speak. As economic conditions improve, people move from camps to houses, but the pressures to continue boarding family, workers, or newcomers to the community is great, so even separate houses have the same characteristics as the apartments in Indiantown.

Work is an area where identity is just now beginning to emerge. As with any new group, low-paid, difficult jobs such as field work or construction were among the first jobs the Maya could get. Conflict arose during the first years in the citrus orchards, where taller, more experienced Mexican and Mexican-American migrant workers quickly outworked the

Maya. Likewise, because sugar cane in Florida is harvested by workers imported from the Caribbean, this kind of work was unavailable to the Maya. In the early 1980s, a few Maya went to the sugar cane fields near Indiantown and Belle Glade to look for work, but were told that they could not work there.

Winter vegetables and citrus proved to be the first and easiest employment sector to enter. Winter vegetable work is highly labor intensive, as crops such as tomatoes, peppers, and the like must be planted, weeded, tended, and harvested. Even before fields are planted, insecticides must be put on the soil, which is then covered with huge sheets of plastic. Maya women are often hired to roll up the plastic after the pesticides have been allowed to stand on the soil. This kind of labor makes them especially susceptible to pesticide poisoning. Few other farm laborers will roll up the plastic, preferring to stay in jobs with less risk. This identification of job and worker has created a Maya identity in the 1980s as one involving risk and danger. Nurses and physicians at hospitals throughout Florida are aware of this aspect of Maya identity. Health workers regularly ask me if the number of birth defects among Maya women in the state is related to the kind of dangerous farm labor they do.

Although the majority of families have resorted to farm and migrant work, a new pattern of work identity is emerging in the community. Some refugees have found work in commercial nurseries and in golf course construction, where their careful attention to agricultural detail has earned them a reputation as excellent employees. One refugee reported that he recently moved to Fort Myers on the other side of the state to work in a commercial nursery. Since he began working there, the nursery owner has hired several other Maya people because he has come to think of them as good workers.

A fledgling textile cooperative has begun in Indiantown, transferring to the United States setting a particularly Maya mode of organization. Using Guatemalan weavings as accessories to women's dresses and skirts, it capitalizes on traditional Maya designs and fabrics. The cooperative was begun by a Catholic nun experienced in textile cooperatives in South America. As yet it has not developed a strong Maya tendency in its organizational structure, other than the interest of Maya men in working there so that traditional men's shoulder bags could be sewn and used here in the United States. The area of San Miguel was not known for its textiles, although men traditionally made shoulder bags for their own use. In the 1970s several cooperatives were developed in the area, although most were agricultural and not artisan cooperatives. The cooperative in Indiantown holds out a promise to the employees of year-round work and a healthy work environment. The difficulties of breaking into merchandising have kept the cooperative small, with only fifteen to thirty employees.

A home industry that has emerged among Maya women in Indiantown has been the making of crocheted bags, often with the colors of the Guatemalan flag and the word "Guatemala" on them. The use of Guatemala as an emblem is a response to the fact that Indiantown designates Maya as Guatemalans. As with other ethnic groups in the United States, the Maya have been labeled by their country of origin and are thus seen as being structurally similar to Haitians, Mexicans, Puerto Ricans, and other Central Americans. The term "Guatemalan" is used as a source of pride among some Guatemalan Maya and non-Maya, but school children say that it is an invective. "They call us 'watermelons,'" one child told me, "because the word sounds like 'Guatemalan.' I don't like it."

The social role of the midwife, an important traditional medical agent in Guatemalan Maya communities (Paul and Paul, 1975), is also important in Indiantown. As Maria Rocha (1991a) showed in her study of midwives and women's health in Indiantown, women who pursue this occupation do so with a sense of pride and tradition. Training in midwifery existed in Guatemala both at traditional levels and through government training and certification. Midwives who come to the United States are proud of their official training certification in Guatemala and find it difficult to understand why their credentials are not honored in the United States. Pregnant Maya women do go to clinics and hospitals to give birth, but the midwives are important promoters of prenatal health and nutrition and will advise women to visit prenatal clinics in the community. In addition, the midwives perform traditional massages, which have both psychological and therapeutic value for women. Maya midwives are known among the women of the community, but the practice of assisting at birth is illegal. As a result, they are at risk of being reported to state health officials. Their work has begun to shift from birth assistants to prenatal health experts in the community, so as to lessen their vulnerability.

The proximity of the beaches of South Florida to Indiantown has meant that construction work is a viable alternative to agricultural labor for Maya men. Younger men are more likely to go into construction work since it requires more English-language skills than does farm labor.

As we have seen, the Maya tend to stay in either agriculture or agriculturally related employment such as the nursery industry. They have not developed the plethora of economic strategies of other immigrants, such as Haitians, and their identity and preference is for work where careful husbandry of plants is valued. While it seems odd to see Maya working on the world-class PGA golf courses near West Palm Beach, their employment there is an aspect of their internal and external identity in the United States.

Leadership patterns are also important to Maya identity. No equivalent of the political leadership structure of the civil-religious hierarchy so common in Guatemala has emerged. Of course, the classic civil-religious hierarchies described by anthropologists in the 1950s and 1960s (Camara 1952, Cancian 1965) had already been transformed in Guatemala by the 1980s (Nash 1989). Still, the responsibilities of sponsoring fiestas, being in charge of particular saints, and taking an active leadership role in community events continued up to the years of violence in Guatemala. When questioned about this, one refugee noted simply that in Indiantown the Maya are guests; they have to ask permission for everything they do. In Guatemala they are the officials of the towns.

One area where leadership can be seen emerging is in the organization of meetings and the process of consensus-building during the planning of the fiesta of San Miguel. As we saw in Chapter Three, the festival began as an event sponsored by the Catholic church. But each year Maya people took a larger role in the organization of the fiesta, until it was taken over completely by one family, the Gonzalezes, in the late 1980s. The "committee of the fiesta" has grown every year in number and authority so that the activities of the fiesta have become more and more Maya. A plethora of smaller committees for entertainment, sports, and queens have been added. Leadership within the committees is exercised through consensus decisions, and the patronal festival has emerged each year with more success.

Both men and women participate in meetings for the planning of the fiesta, and a characteristically Maya sociolinguistic structure of decision making is used (Burns 1980). A topic is first brought out by one of the visible leaders or committee directors. A free-ranging discussion ensues, with many people talking at once and no attention given to any one person. After five or ten minutes of such polyphonic conversation, people quiet down and someone sums up the decision of the group. Outsiders, such as church workers or non-Maya visitors, find the process difficult to follow, confused by the absence of turn-taking based on Western ideas of hierarchy and rules of order. Maya task groups, such as storytelling groups, corn-growing groups, and marimba bands, share an ethic of cooperation and rotating leadership. When I first heard Maya marimba music, I was impressed with how much cooperation was needed just to get through a song. Five players sometimes play the same marimba, standing next to one another with two or four rubber-tipped sticks in their hands. When one player becomes tired, another will walk up and take his place so that the music can continue for up to twelve hours at a time. Likewise, my own work with Maya language in everyday use (Burns 1983) led me to appreciate the skill of simultaneous narrators in completing a myth or story. Conversations, storytelling, and marimba playing are events where turn-taking is an activity engaged in by many people at once. Unlike my own tradition where people make an effort to attain their own individual status, Maya social organization is based on the value of several people working alongside one another in a kind of social polyphony.

Besides recalling their home village in Guatemala, the fiesta of San Miguel signals those Maya who have entered the migrant stream to return to the area of Indiantown. As such, it has become an important event in the public lives of the people. For many the festival is an occasion when they can socialize with each other, not doing anything more than standing around in small groups and quietly visiting. It is also a time to put on a public show for Maya and non-Maya alike that stresses the identity of Maya people. Traditional clothing is worn, children are taught to dance to marimba music, and the queens of the fiesta work hard to prepare speeches in Maya, Spanish, and English. As the fiesta has evolved, the cultural activities have become more North American, with booths, raffles, and the incorporation of other ethnic groups in the events; but even so, the fiesta leadership has managed to create an event that is definitely Maya.

One year included a surprise moment of fiesta revitalization. At the end of the second day of the fiesta a group of masked and costumed dancers came out and danced to traditional marimba music. Masked dances, such as the Dance of the Conquest, or in this case, the Dance of the Elders, are important features of patronal festivals in Guatemala. True, the masks were purchased from a K-Mart discount store rather than being made of papier-mâché, but the dance still exemplified a confidence in Maya identity that had not been exhibited in previous years. One refugee brought out a video camcorder to record the event.

Leadership for women in the community has evolved through the enactment of the festival as well. Both men and women are masters of ceremonies during the events. One of the first queens of the festival, Eulalia Santiago, was hired by the Catholic diocese of West Palm Beach to work in the diocesan office for migrant workers. Eulalia took the post after first working as a public school aide in Indiantown. In her position in West Palm Beach, she has developed into a spokesperson for the Maya community in general and has established herself within a network of social service agencies in South Florida.

Less-public positions of leadership among Maya women in Indiantown have also begun to develop, even though the rigors of family life in the community make exercising leadership difficult. Women's leadership roles in the context of the Guatemalan insurgency of the 1980s were made very visible through the work of Rigoberta Menchu, whose high-profile indigenous leadership included the publication of an autobiography (Menchu 1984). Maya women in Indiantown do not follow her model of leadership by becoming publicly visible, but they do follow her model by being vocal in meetings of the associations in the community.

The Maya communities of Yucatan are characterized by a pattern of leadership that bridges traditional small-town life and the urban world. These "culture brokers" (Press 1969) are people who are successful in both Maya and world market cultural arenas, but their leadership reflects a high degree of ambiguity and ambivalence. Often they are fluent in Maya, Spanish, and English.

One of these culture brokers, Gaspar Domingo, worked as a Maya and Spanish radio announcer in Guatemala prior to coming to the United States. He quickly learned English and became one of the people called on whenever the press needed a local person for an interview. He also began to speak at local association meetings, such as the Kiwanis Club and the county supervisory commission. Gaspar worked in the winter vegetable fields when he first arrived, then found a position on a golf course construction crew. These jobs gave him continued legitimacy among the other Maya immigrants to Indiantown. He very quickly became the person people went to when they were in trouble, when they needed to find work, or when they needed a translator to help with their tax returns. Gaspar organized a second fiesta in the community, held to honor the Virgin of Ixcoy in July.

As Gaspar became more successful as a broker, gossip about him and his family increased. He complained that people said he was making money off the community. Other men in the community told me that Gaspar believed that he was the only real spokesperson for the community and presented a one-sided view of what was happening there. "He talks as if we are all Indian," one said to me, "but we are not. Most of us in Indiantown are Guatemalans, not Indians." This identification with the country rather than the community of birth reflects the wider community identification of the immigrants as Guatemalans, and it also shows how the choice of a national or local community identity can be used as a point of intra-community conflict when culture brokers rise to leadership positions.

Gaspar spent several years in an ambivalent state. He enjoyed being able to interact with the helping or social service community of Indiantown; being able, with his wife, to socialize his three children through the Kanjobal Maya language; and being promoted to foreman of his golf course construction crew. But his life was very public. If he missed a Sunday mass, the local priest would ask him about it, as he sang in the choir. If he didn't open his door to people at all hours of the day or night, he was criticized for not helping everyone equally. He hated the criticism, the gossip, and the factions of the community. Still, he could not just stop being a culture broker. He was, in a way, a prisoner of the culture-broker model of leadership that had developed in the community.

Religion is an area where Maya identity challenges stereotypes about Guatemalan peasants. In terms of identity, religious heterogeneity characterizes the Maya in Florida, not religious homogeneity. As the Maya people have spread into other areas of the state, religion has been one factor: Adventists, for example, are more likely to be found in West Palm Beach while Catholics remain in Indiantown.

The Catholic church in Indiantown has been an important ally to the Maya in their quest for political and social asylum in South Florida. The activist priest from the parish who was heard from earlier in this work, Frank O'Loughlin, was known throughout the migrant streams of the state as an advocate and defender of undocumented aliens. Migrant workers besides the Maya remember religious services in the church early in the decade that included practicing what to do during immigration raids. The prestige of the Catholic church in Indiantown and its welcoming of the Maya led to a resumption of Catholic religious affiliation among many of the Maya immigrants. The

Saturday evening services were held in Spanish with Maya gospel readings by people like Gaspar Domingo. Attendance at the Saturday mass became one of the few opportunities for Maya people to congregate in large numbers and speak their language. Attendance at the weekly mass did not translate into a complete acceptance of the Catholic religion, however. Marriages in the church of Maya couples was rare, even though many marriages took place in the community.

While Catholicism is an important part of the lives of many Maya, even to the extent that the grounds of the church are used for the annual patronal festival, the Maya are not all Catholic. Of eighty-nine Indiantown families surveyed by Maria Miralles (1986), only 36 percent reported being Catholic. The others were split among Seventh-Day Adventists and other Protestant groups (37 percent) and a surprisingly large number (27 percent) who replied that they did not follow any religion. The large contingent of Protestants reflects the tremendous increase in fundamentalist religions in Guatemala throughout the 1960s and 1970s (Brintnall 1979). These people attend events along with the rest of the community but are more and more separate because of their weekly trips to West Palm Beach to attend services. The large number who did not report a religious affiliation include those who practice traditional *costumbre,* or Maya religion, as well as those who may have learned to deny their religious affiliation in order to avoid being singled out for violence. This group also reflects the process of "de-conversion," or the move away from evangelical sects in Mexico and Guatemala, that characterizes the 1990s. As a kind of strategic adaptation to the political and religious changes in Guatemala, many people who converted to Protestant groups and the Catholic Action movement in the 1960s and 1970s reverted to a mix of official but seldom-practiced Catholicism and *costumbre* in the 1980s.

Maya communication strategies have been a positive way to express identity in South Florida. Playing the marimba has been one of the most visible manifestations. The marimba is used in Maya family ceremonies such as baptisms and birthdays and is also used for communitywide celebrations such as the patronal fiesta of San Miguel. The marimba has also become a positive marker of identity beyond the community. The Maya marimba musicians played at the United States Folk Festival in Washington, D.C., in 1985 to exemplify endangered folk tradition. Since then, they have played throughout Florida and many other states at festivals, Indian pow-wows, and university campuses.

The marimba has tremendous value internal to the community as a marker of identity and emotion. The marimba attracts young people who want to learn music that is considered truly Maya. It is common to hear people express strong emotional attachment to marimba music. At a meeting of the CORN-Maya association in June 1991, the audience was asked what they thought the association should accomplish in the future. Raul Guzman, a young man in his early twenties, stood up and said, "We should play more marimba music. I believe that music is the most important thing in our lives, and the community here needs to hear more of it so that we can be reminded of who we are."

The Maya language continues to flourish, even as people in Indiantown learn Spanish from their Mexican co-workers and housemates and English in schools and other institutions. In 1988 the preschool teacher of the town noted that out of eighteen new Maya children in her class, thirteen spoke only Maya. In the annual patronal festival, the queens of the fiesta each give a speech first in Maya, then in Spanish, and finally in English.

There are no formal attempts in the community to maintain Maya through media or education, which makes Maya language retention even more remarkable. The Maya people are faced with shopping in English, learning about work in Spanish, English, and sometimes Maya, watching television in English, seeking help from English-speaking police, lawyers, and social service workers, and hearing English around them in the community. But Maya continues to be the principal means of communication, even with such a strong push toward new languages. Cassette tapes sent back and forth from Guatemala with news from both the United States and the homeland contribute to the strength of indigenous language. Also, Maya political asylum seekers have insisted that their cases be heard in Maya so as to be sure that the stories of their political persecution could be told. Speaking Maya continues to be a communicative marker of identity in Indiantown, not only because of the connection of the language to the refugees' home villages in Guatemala, but also because of the contemporary importance of the Maya language in the social and political contexts of Indiantown.

Besides being an element of self-image, Maya identity is also an external feature of the new immigrants' life in South Florida. As we have seen, the image of the Maya has shifted from one of victims undergoing culture shock to one of sometimes dangerous migrant farmworkers. Increasingly, younger, single men are arriving in the community without families to constrain their leisure behavior. Weekend drinking has become the most common recreation for them. In addition, the sheer numbers of refugees as well as other migrants working in the area has stretched the carrying capacity of the community to its limits. Housing, transportation, health care, waste disposal, and the schools have all been inundated by the tremendous influx of immigrants to this unincorporated community.

Maya ethnic identity is tied to the circumstances of their arrival as refugees. When they first came to Indiantown, their appearance provoked an outpouring of sympathy and concern. Here were whole families with children whose blistered feet and anemic state told of a flight from terror. The fact that they were modern-day Maya people also forged their identity in the United States. Few people in the area of Indiantown knew that the Maya civilization still existed. Those who did and knew the state of Guatemalan violence saw these first refugees as people from a proud Maya past—a viewpoint exemplified by photographic books such as *Guatemala: Eternal Spring, Eternal Tyranny*, by Jean-Marie Simon (1987). An early newspaper account portrayed this first Maya identity in Indiantown: "In a migrant labor camp here, Gloria, a two-year-old Mayan Indian, plays with a pay phone. She smiles as she lifts the receiver off the hook and holds it to her ear. Back in the isolated mountain town of San Miguel, Guatemala, where her parents lived until 1982, there are only a few private phones. Most rural homes have no electricity or running water" (Christian Science *Monitor*, May 28, 1985:7).

The Catholic church in Indiantown became an advocate for farmworker rights and migrant workers in general prior to the coming of the Maya. The appearance of the Maya was fortunate for the efforts of the church. The Maya were very visible because of the uniqueness of their heritage and were easily represented as victims of Central American politics and as exploited workers here in the United States.

Outside Indiantown, during the first several months after their arrival, the Maya were unknown. At a flea market in a nearby town, many people surveyed did not know that their customers were Maya refugees from Guatemala. One manager who was interviewed speculated that the Maya people were from the Far East, perhaps the Philippines, since they didn't speak Spanish and looked different from the Mexican and Central American farmworkers who often came to the market on weekends.

A few years later, the Maya became known as Guatemalan—not Maya—undocumented aliens. A series of letters to the local newspaper documents this shift. The letters were prompted by an accident in which a carload of young Maya men drove through a local resident's yard, destroying the lawn and flowers. The resident wrote to the local paper to express her outrage:

> Most of those people do not know what laws are, let alone abide by them. Where are they a credit to our community? When they are pushing us aside at the post office to mail their $500+ money orders to Guatemala? . . . or living a dozen people to one house? BEWARE: The Guatemalan Tornado is on the road again. Next time it might be your yard, your house, or worse, your child. Thanks again for letting me express my anger and frustration resulting from the damages incurred at my residence caused by a drunk Guatemalan. (Indiantown *News*, June 24, 1987)

It is important to note that the resident makes several comments that reflect a dramatic shift in labeling from the earlier report. First, the people are Guatemalans in this letter, not Maya. Second, they are unaware of laws; they are "outside" normal society. Third, they are depicted as affecting the "balance of payments" and deficit by sending United States money away. Fourth, they are described as socially uncontrolled because of the way they live and drink.

Another writer to the newspaper complained the following week: "I can see [that] the influx of Guatemalans and Mexicans has dropped the value of property over fifty percent" (Indiantown *News*, June 30, 1987). Here the Maya people were identified along with other Hispanics in the community, an identification that led to a counterresponse:

> The editorial column is starting to become a column of hatred. It is now being directed to racism, especially on His-

panics and Guatemalans. . . . If it weren't for all these migrant people picking crops you would not have all the fruit
and vegetables at the supermarkets. You American people
sure wouldn't get your buns out in the hot sun and labor in
the fields all day. Wake up, criticizers, and stop judging
races. We pay taxes the same as you. (Indiantown *News*,
July 6, 1987)

The newspaper quickly stepped in with an editorial asking
its readers to refrain from continuing the outpouring of both
anger and pride about the Maya refugees in the community.
Many residents worried that the letters gave Indiantown an
image as a community of bigots. After a few weeks the Maya
themselves began to joke at their new identity: they began
referring to a Maya person behind the wheel of a car as a "Guatemalan tornado."

When Oliver La Farge worked in the Kanjobal area of Guatemala in the 1920s, he noted that the Kanjobal drank heavily. He
said, though, that "one would hesitate to remove the bottle
from them until the entire pattern of their lives is changed.
They are . . . eternally chafing under the yoke of conquest, and
never for a moment forgetting that they are a conquered people.
In occasional drunkenness . . . they find a much needed release"
(La Farge 1947:100). If local residents or social workers are
asked what they see as the principal problem with the Kanjobal people today, they will usually say drunkenness. One of
the parish priests who was given the Indiantown post after
Frank O'Loughlin left equated beer drinking with prostitution
during his homily during the patronal festival mass, exhorting
people to reach for a can of Coca-Cola instead of beer when they
were tempted to drink. Maya people themselves see the deplor-
able effects of drinking on their families, work, and status in
South Florida. Those Maya who are Seventh-Day Adventists

and members of other Protestant denominations do not drink. But as La Farge noted, the Maya live under the yoke of conquest. That is a feature of their identity that has persisted here in the United States, seasoned over five hundred years of experience.

Maya identity in the community today is being tempered through interethnic communication and conflict. The Maya maintain a precarious existence in Indiantown while they wait to return to Guatemala or to make their new lives here. Throughout the 1980s, as many studies documented (Manz 1988, 1989; Washington Office on Latin America 1988; Painter 1987; AVANCSO 1990), returning to Guatemala for more than short visits was not a real option. In the meantime, the Maya refugees of Florida are in the process of creating a new identity. That identity is now based on life in a small U.S. migrant town, and so partakes of the issues and conflicts that other migrant workers face. In a booklet of poems, stories, and even a play written by students in 1987, put together by the local middle school, one Maya student condensed his experiences into a short story that summarizes the emergence of identity described in this chapter:

I lived in a town that's called San Miguel. Everything was fine. Then my dad worked in California picking apples. I lived with my grandpa and grandma and my brother and sister in Guatemala. They had a big farm. There you can pick corn and beans. There were no phones in the houses. I went to kindergarten when I was seven in San Miguel. My aunt had a big store. We always had a lot to eat. We helped pick the vegetables. I had to work with my grandpa. Then I didn't get to go back to school. Sometimes we sold corn in the town. I was 9 years old when the government soldiers came into San Miguel. They had guns and they lived there a long time. They think that the villagers started the war.

The soldiers killed a lot of villagers. The guerrillas wanted
to kill the soldiers of the government. I was afraid of both
of them because when they came to San Miguel, they
wanted to kill my grandpa. They were thinking that my
grandpa was the boss of the guerrillas, and they thought my
grandpa started the war with them. The guerrillas wanted
to kill the government soldiers because they wouldn't pay
for the crops that much, only 50 cents a day. In American
money, it's only 10 cents. They would come into people's
houses at night and kill the men. My grandpa had to go
somewhere else to sleep every night so they would not find
him. We were sad because my grandpa wasn't there every
night. The men were safe during the day because they were
at work until 6 o'clock at night. Everyone went inside. My
dad came to a town called Huehuetenango. Then he mailed
a letter to grandpa that he was coming to get us. Grandpa
took us to my dad. We paid for a car to take us. Then we
went to eat some food and we went to a hotel and got some
sleep. About 8 o'clock in the morning, my dad rented a car
in Mexico, and we got a guy that crossed us to this side of
the United States. Then we went in a truck. He had papers
for the United States. First we made a plan. We hid in a big
box in the truck. When we got to Arizona, we hid in the
trees. In the morning we walked with the man who helped
us. We paid him about $150 dollars in American money. We
walked 15 hours to a city. We met another man in a van. He
took us to the airport. We paid $170. My dad bought tickets
to West Palm Beach. My stepmother met us in West Palm
Beach. We paid a friend to get us at the airport. I was happy
to get here. It was Sunday, Mother's Day, May 10, 1984. No-
body will kill me here. We came to Indiantown. My dad got
a job cutting cabbage. It was hard because we didn't know
what people were saying. We had to learn English to come

to school. The Americans were good to us. They liked us because there were just a few of us, not like now. I went to Warfield, but they sent me to Indiantown Middle School because I was 11 years old. I wouldn't want to go back to Guatemala. We have more things here and more money, and the food here tastes better.

While forms of identity are expanding in complexity, the rigors of migrant work, the lack of opportunities for the Maya to work together as a community, and the lessening prospects for a return to Guatemala have changed Maya identity in terms of others in the community. Scudder and Colson (1982) discussed stages in forced migration as a sequence of activities including recruitment, transition, development, and incorporation. In the case of the Maya, few of these stages have been passed. The Maya have been in a period of transition since arriving in Indiantown in 1982. The arrival of new refugees and families of those already in the community has precluded a shift to incorporation in the town, except as migrant workers. Indiantown has provided the Maya with a relatively safe haven, but it has not provided them with an economically or socially satisfying context within which to thrive. The Maya came to Indiantown as unusual people from a culture thought to have vanished. They are now seen as just another group of migrant workers, exhibiting behavior that is sometimes offensive and threatening to many non-Maya people in the community.

SEVEN

VISUAL ANTHROPOLOGY AND THE MAYA

"Can you make a video about Indiantown?" asked Jerónimo Camposeco when we first met. The release of the commercial film *El Norte* in the mid-1980s was well known among the Maya community, as it was based on interviews with people who had first come to California and later to Florida. Television news teams made many visits to the town—so many that after a few years people began refusing to be interviewed on camera. One of the first "media events" that the community witnessed was the helicopter landing of a television news team in Indiantown in the early 1980s. Although other school children ran out to see the landing of the helicopter, the Guatemalan Maya children were frightened that the helicopter was part of an army attack on their newfound home of Indiantown. They hid under their desks in school and refused even to talk about their fear.

In the spring of 1985 filmmaker Alan Saperstein and I produced a documentary on the community, *Maya in Exile*. This documentary was followed by a second, *Maya Fiesta*, in 1988, in which we attempted to portray the cultural side of life in Indiantown for the Guatemala Maya. In 1991 I produced two educational videotapes directed at facilitating clinic use among Guatemalan women, *Salud Entre Dos Culturas* (Health Between

Two Cultures) (Rocha 1991b) and *La Mujer Maya: Salud Maternal* (The Maya Woman: Maternal Health). *Salud Entre Dos Culturas* was made with Maria Cecilia Rocha (1991b), whose master of arts thesis on the community (1991a) formed the basis for the production. *La Mujer Maya* was made with a physician's assistant and public health specialist, Randi Cameon (1991), with funding provided by the March of Dimes Birth Defects Foundation. This chapter discusses how these video programs were made and the collaboration that went into them. The way we made the first program, *Maya in Exile*, illustrates the issues and problems of doing ethnographic video.

Cameras, camcorders, cassette recorders, and VCRs are common throughout Indiantown and the Maya community there. VCRs, along with televisions, are one of the first consumer items purchased by new Maya families, and the trade in Mexican videotapes is brisk throughout Indiantown and other migrant worker communities. Baptisms, festivals, soccer games, and marriages are photographed and videotaped whenever possible by those Maya who have purchased cameras. Photographs of these events are put on walls and sent to friends and family in other communities. The Maya of Indiantown are interested in television and pictures and see both individual and community uses for visual products. Professional photographers and television crews who come to Indiantown find that the Maya immigrants are sophisticated with regard to the techniques and uses of their trade.

Professional film and video has followed the tradition in photography of making a conceptual distinction between the subjects in front of the camera and the professionals behind it. But visual anthropologists have argued that such a separation is not always useful or even necessary today. The subjects of photography, film, and video are capable of using cameras, making decisions about editing and presentation, and distributing professional work. This is the case with the Maya of Indiantown, who have a history of using the electronic media themselves. As video cameras become less and less expensive, it is common to see camcorders in the hands of people like the Maya, who now document their own celebrations. Consequently, the video productions carried out in Indiantown have been based on collaboration informed by the Maya's interest in and knowledge of video and audio cassette recording.

Visual anthropology is the use of photography, film, and other images to study and present cultural situations and processes throughout the world. The study of images is one part of visual anthropology and the making of documentaries, whether still or moving, is another. The study of images includes those taken by an anthropologist with still or film cameras as well as those created by others, including indigenous communities. The analysis of the images that are created within communities has brought visual anthropology close to the study of the graphic arts around the world, as indigenous people have not had access to cameras and film until relatively recently. In the 1960s and early 1970s, however, Sol Worth and John Adair trained Navajo people in the use of motion picture equipment (Worth and Adair 1970). They found that the Navajo quickly learned the techniques of film production and editing. When the films of Navajo life were reviewed, it was apparent that the "language" of the film was Navajo. Decisions about what to film, the construction of sequences of time in a film, and the conventions associated with characters and places were based on the Navajo language more than on any universal features of what is often called "the language of film." Worth and Adair's work with the Navajo has relevance to our own work in Indiantown in that it shows the importance of turning to ideas of culture to understand the filmmaking process. While the videos in Indiantown are not modeled after the Navajo project, they do use Worth and Adair's approach of understanding the process of production as primarily a cultural one.

Robert Ziller (1990) has taken this approach even farther by developing a technique of "auto photography" to explore issues of social psychology. Ziller provides inexpensive cameras to photographically naive people in many parts of the world and asks them to tell with photographs "who they are." Ziller's contention, that the act of recording social and psychological information through a camera demands a greater degree of attention than writing with paper and pencil, was an important feature of the video work in Indiantown. In effect, we were working together with Maya assistants to tell "who they were" through video images. But unlike Ziller's, our approach has been collaborative; we worked alongside people in the community, eliciting their ideas on what to record with the camera, using their own photographs in the projects, and combining their talents with ours to produce the projects.

The separation of naive photography from professional photography and video production is increasingly being replaced by collaboration between indigenous people and professionals. In Australia, a team of indigenous people and filmmakers/anthropologists have collaborated to make a series of successful television documentaries about aboriginal law and custom (Michaels and Kelly 1986). Although Worth and Adair's work with the Navajo illustrates the ease with which native people could learn the technical aspects of filmmaking and editing, Michaels and Kelly's report on Australian collaboration shows the value of professionals and local people working together in creating video programs, to the mutual benefit of both. The programs made by Michaels and Kelly in Australia as a part of the Australian Institute of Aboriginal Studies project reflect not only the importance of local subject matter to the collaborative team but also the changes in crew organization that occur when the lines between the filmmakers and the film subjects are blurred.

Visual anthropology used to be defined as the production of programs or documentaries to be used in classrooms or the world of television. Margaret Mead, in one of her last articles about the field of anthropology, argued that anthropology had been so steeped in the tradition of the written word that acceptance of visual materials was usually met with distrust (Mead 1975). Mead's interest in visual anthropology was long-standing, evidenced by her use of photography and film in her Balinese personality studies (Bateson and Mead 1941) as well as her appearances on film and television near the end of her career.

The advent of inexpensive video cameras and video recorders in the 1980s and 1990s has meant that more and more work in general anthropology is being done with video. Many of the beliefs about visual anthropology remain tied to the commercial production of "ethnographic films," as Heider (1976) describes them, especially by those scholars who have pioneered the use of documentary films in anthropology (Rollwagen 1988). But the use of video as a part of the fieldwork "took kit" of ethnographers is gaining interest and following (Collier and Collier 1986). The applied anthropology of education has been an area where video note-taking and visual anthropology have become more widely accepted. Yucatec Maya schools were studied by Stearns (1986), using video recordings of the events in the classrooms. Stearns recorded the daily teaching activities and then showed them to parents at night to elicit their perceptions of the cultural context of bilingual education in Maya and Spanish (Stearns 1986).

Between the use of home camcorders to record aspects of fieldwork and professional documentary films are documentaries that are locally relevant and yet professionally produced. Unlike using video or still photography as a note-taking device, this use of the media aims at producing a final program that is directed at public audiences. The first documentary on the Indiantown community, *Maya in Exile,* is an example of a video in this local production mode.

I began developing a documentary video project to interpret the Maya experience in the unusual context of life in Indiantown. One impetus for the creation of a documentary on Indiantown was the commercial film *El Norte,* about the journey of a Guatemalan brother and sister from their homeland to Los Angeles. Some of the Maya of Florida resented the film because it divulged the name of a prominent Maya family who had immigrated to the United States. They and others felt that relatives still in Guatemala had been put at risk through the widespread showing of the film in both the United States and Guatemala.

The making of the video *Maya in Exile* and the subsequent video programs in the community has been a cooperative effort to interpret the revitalization of a Maya community outside the Maya homeland of Guatemala. Looking at the process will help us to see the issues and problems that the project faced.

The making of *Maya in Exile* was accomplished by consciously adopting a fluid, small-group approach to the project. In many ethnographic films and documentaries, a lone anthropologist either made or contracted with a professional filmmaker to make a record of village ceremonies and rituals, often in exotic and dangerous places.

The relationships between anthropologists and filmmakers has sometimes been cordial and complementary, as described by Asch (1979). When the Yanomamo films were made in the late 1960s and 1970s, Asch collaborated with anthropologist Napoleon Chagnon, who had lived with the Yanomamo for some time. Asch was amazed at the difficult conditions when he arrived in the field as a contracted filmmaker. His skill at photographing the visual dimensions of Chagnon's analysis of alliance formation in Yanomamo villages make his work an example of how filmmakers and anthropologists can work together well. The roles of the filmmaker and the anthropologist were well defined in the project.

But many anthropologists report that filmmakers, like their journalist cousins, are pushy, arrogant, and difficult to work with. And filmmakers contend that anthropologists are wordy, overly cautious, and too tied up in their own academic worlds to understand the language of film. Howard Becker (1975) said that photographers and sociologists are suspicious of each other, and as a result the differences between the world of photography and the world of anthropology often become exaggerated on documentary projects. Hubert Smith's collaboration with an anthropolgist on a series of films on the modern Yucatec Maya (1979) was fraught with problems. Smith found that he and the ethnographer could not get along, and conflicts over using the vehicle, how to compensate the people, and what to film overtook their relationship. Smith even edited out the anthropologist in his four-hour series of films *The Living Maya* (1985).

Of course neither of these working relationships, cordial or stilted, takes into account the subjects of documentary work and how they work with filmmakers or anthropologists. When we made *Maya in Exile*, the Maya principle of small-group organization guided the structure of planning and videotaping. It seemed appropriate to use this form of social organization in making the video, as it would allow for participation by Maya associates that reflected their own organizational behavior.

Making a video, like any anthropological project, is an exercise in small-group behavior. Anthropologists often view families and households as the only small group standing between the individual and large groups such as organizations and kinship groups. But small groups are critical organizations in societies, whether they are friendship circles, work groups, or music groups like the marimba band of Indiantown. The marimba band members of Indiantown play expertly without hitting each other's sticks or stepping on each other's toes. Their interaction seemed to be a model of how a video team could work. Likewise, the Maya of Indiantown also used a polyphonic storytelling tradition that was very similar to what I had found in Yucatec Maya society. It seemed that these expressive activities shared a common small-group structure that could easily be transferred to the expressive activity of making a film. The professional video and film people who were brought into the project were willing to work in this mode, as the democratic and fluid nature of the small group was in keeping with their own work habits.

One of the interesting features of Maya small groups such as the marimba group is the way in which leadership is exercised. The groups are loosely structured, and leaders emerge to suit a particular song or playing technique. There are no overall "band leaders," but rather experts in different categories of music, such as religious or secular music, or music from one village or another. When our documentary group was formed, we sought to imitate both the cooperation seen in the actual playing of the marimba and the enactment of leadership positions found there. We did this because we recognized that although each of us had different skills, these skills overlapped and complemented each other. The documentary could be made only if we shifted from a Western European individual orientation to a Maya task-group orientation and submerged our occupational specializations and egos in favor of the project.

The way we worked can be illustrated by outlining a portion of the history of the project. When I met Jerónimo in 1983, he came to one of my classes at the University of Florida and made an eloquent plea for stopping the genocide and ethnocide that was occurring in Guatemala. Guatemala and the diaspora of hundreds of thousands of Maya people was not treated very much in the media, and so his talk was surprising and even astonishing to students.

One of the students in the class, Greg MacDonald, talked with Jerónimo and me after the class about what he could do to help. Greg decided to drop out of school to work in Indiantown for the next six months as a volunteer. He began working at a Catholic social service agency, El Centro, taking people to immigration hearings, helping them out at the hospital, and learning about the issues that faced the community. Greg became one of the major researchers on the documentary; he was instrumental in establishing our credibility in the community when we came down to film and was especially important in arranging for filming in the houses of the families that had become his friends while he lived in the town. Greg also had an archive of still photographs that he had taken during his work in the community, which were used in the story board for the documentary.

When Jerónimo and I talked about the topics of videotape, we first discussed the uses of the tape. The videotape was planned to address several specific problems and so was an applied anthropology project. It was planned to entertain and enlighten; but more importantly, it was designed to advocate for the Maya in Indiantown.

The first and most obvious problem the documentary intended to explore was the ethnocide—the destruction of cultural knowledge, practice, and ways of transmitting the ideas of Maya society—that accompanied the violence in Guatemala and the exile of the Maya. The dispersion of the Maya and their presence in the United States led to profound cultural shock at both the individual and community levels. Within the Maya community, the Maya homelands of Guatemala are now only a memory recalled when a relative sends an audio cassette tape bearing news of family life or continuing problems. The Maya people are faced with learning English and learning migrant work as a means of physical survival. From outside the community, the people of Indiantown appear to be like any other poor migrant group. They are seen as mere farmworkers, people marginal to mainstream United States culture. So one of our first goals was to make a video that would be accessible to a public audience and would prompt them to look beyond the present occupation these people have as farmworkers and to recognize the thousands of years of Mayan tradition that they carry. Likewise, a documentary video showing the continuance of Maya tradition in the strange surroundings of a South Florida migrant community would be useful within the Maya community as an affirmation and celebration of their way of life even as they struggled with daily survival and the fear of being deported.

The second problem the video was designed to meet was fund-raising. Political asylum requires that the Maya take part in two- or three-year court proceedings to present their cases. Jerónimo had been on many speaking tours to churches, schools, and other groups in order to raise funds for legal assistance to the community. We decided to sell the video at a very low cost so that it would have a wide distribution. Any funds gained from the sale would go directly to legal and social assistance programs already operating in the community.

A third problem was related to the second. Jerónimo and others who work with refugees find that there is a great demand for speaking engagements, often so many that trips and talks can become an exhausting addition to the everyday work of legal and social assistance. We hoped that *Maya in Exile* could be used in place of a speaker or be sent out ahead of time to prepare an audience for more detailed and fruitful discussions.

Making a documentary film or video is enormously expensive. As a rule of thumb, filmmakers budget about fifteen hundred dollars per minute as a way of pricing out a production. Thus, a one-hour documentary is normally budgeted at ninety thousand dollars. Like many applied anthropology projects, *Maya in Exile* was developed from the grass-roots level without major foundation or commercial funding. Yet at the same time we felt that the project should be done well and as quickly as possible. People were being called for immigration hearings from the community, the violence in Guatemala continued, and the U.S. State Department was telling news reporters that all Maya refugees should return home. During the spring of 1985 Indiantown was the subject of a number of short news clips on the major commercial networks. In keeping with the idea of "balance," a minute and a half of footage shot in Indiantown was often balanced with reports from State Department officials who said that returning refugees were welcome in Guatemala and would be resettled in "model villages" far from the violence associated with the rebel movement. This was contrary to the experience of the few Maya people who did return to Guatemala during this time, who found that the "model villages" were places where civil rights were routinely ignored (Manz 1988). We felt that these statements and other "quick and dirty" news reports needed to be balanced by a more careful documentary based on the issues as they appeared to the Maya in the community.

We were not able to raise the kind of funds needed to make the video within the tradition of mainstream filmmaking. Grants from institutions or foundations required too long a waiting period for our group, and the immigration of Maya people to the United States was not as intriguing to agencies that funded films and videos as were the Maya in their homelands. We used two strategies to overcome this difficulty. First, we found people who were willing to donate time and professional equipment for the project. Second, we raised funds as we went along through direct solicitation and other means. These two strategies allowed us to reduce costs and still complete the project within a relatively short time period of six months.

The director and co-producer of the documentary, Alan Saperstein, had studied anthropology as an undergraduate, but had gone on to a professional career as a filmmaker and television producer at a public television station. He was familiar with the tradition of ethnographic filming and had a network of friends in the film and video business to draw upon. We met when I was a guest on a local talk show that he directed. Soon afterward we began discussing the project. He was fascinated with the case and saw it as a way to further his productions on the importance of place in people's lives. *Maya in Exile* gave him an opportunity to work with a socially relevant theme and do some fieldwork in a small Florida town. He was willing to donate his time to the project if his expenses during the videotaping could be met.

Through Alan, several other professional film and video people were brought into the project. The writer and narrator for the documentary, Denise Matthews, was an independent filmmaker from the Northeast who had worked on projects dealing with teenage pregnancy, occupational safety, and rape. While she was planning a film on rural midwifery, she visited Florida and came to see me because of a project I had completed with an African-American women's health cooperative. Denise brought to the project the skills of a videographer, a writer, and a narrator. She continued to be interested in Indiantown and the Maya and worked on several of the subsequent videotapes, including *La Mujer Maya*, on which she worked as videographer and editor.

The videographer on *Maya in Exile* was a Belgian filmmaker, François Pietri, who had been raised in Venezuela. Besides his talents as a filmmaker, he had the additional advantage of being able to speak Spanish. He also had his own broadcast-quality camera and recording equipment, which allowed us to avoid the cost of renting field recording equipment. He was employed in an industrial video studio that later gave us access to editing equipment.

Even with the help of a production team willing to work for the project without pay, we still needed funds to buy tape stock, pay engineers, and meet our expenses while videotaping in Indiantown. To raise these funds we relied on direct solicitation from local Central American support groups, amnesty groups, sanctuary movements, and private individuals. While it is difficult to solicit funds from private individuals for far-off projects, a direct, local project such as this has the appeal of local recognition.

A second way that money was raised for completing the documentary was through preview showings of the first cut of the documentary. We arranged showings in the city where we were doing the editing and advertised it through some of the same groups mentioned earlier, as well as through newspaper advertisements and flyers. Several hundred people came to the showings, enough to raise sufficient funds for the completion of the editing. At that time we also had the advantage of showing the rough cut of the documentary to a highly motivated audience. Their comments and criticisms were important in our decisions for the final edit of the documentary.

We began videotaping in April. We spent a week in the community with the video crew, attempting to record activities in people's homes, in public areas such as laundromats and stores, and in the schools. We were fortunate to be able to record an interview with one man who had just arrived in Florida from Guatemala. He described his journey from Guatemala to Jerónimo, who assisted him in filling out papers for political asylum. Neil Boothby, a psychologist living in the community who works with children of war, offered to let us stay in his house while we were taping in Indiantown. We were able to videotape his work with young Maya, in which he had them draw their experiences to express through images what they had endured in Guatemala.

We were unable to videotape the classrooms in the migrant labor school because we ran out of time. Fortunately, a friend knew one of the national news teams who had been in Indiantown and had videotaped the school the week before we were there. They offered to let us use their footage of the school for our project.

We began editing the videotape in early May. Our deadline for completing the program was the end of June, when the marimba band was due to travel to Washington, D.C. We wanted to have the tapes ready for them to take to the performance. By editing the tape in the evenings and at night, we were able to meet the deadline. The outline for the piece was created through our discussions both while we were videotaping and while we were editing. I wrote out a general outline and text, which was then rewritten by Denise Matthews for editing.

We began the documentary with scenes from a flea market on the coast of Florida where many Maya families go each weekend. The flea market is a place that has enough similarities to markets in Guatemala and Mexico to make people feel comfortable. It provides entertainment and a chance to buy clothes and small appliances, and gives people a change from the cramped houses and apartments of Indiantown. The flea market scenes also provide viewers from the United States with something familiar, and allow them to see the Maya emerging, as it were, from the crowds of people in South Florida.

This first scene, although only a few minutes long, took over eight hours to edit. Each of us argued about which scenes should be used, what the beginning and end points should be, and in what order the scenes should appear. The arguing taught us that the editing process could not be as fluid and involve as many people as the recording part of the work. Within a few days of this first editing decision, everyone but Alan Saperstein and me had given up on helping with the editing.

Following the scene at the flea market, the documentary moves to the house of a young Maya couple, where a psychologist, Neil Boothby, was interviewing a young Maya boy. This is a scene with great emotional impact. The picture the boy drew was of a helicopter flying over the family house, the bullets raining down on a Maya village, and the boy's family watching in the foreground. I wanted to let the scene play for four or five minutes, but Alan felt that people would find it difficult to look at the pictures and hear the interview between Boothby and the boy for that long a time. We ended up using less than three minutes, and interspersed photographs of Guatemala taken by Jerónimo Camposeco throughout the sequence.

The third part of the documentary describes Guatemala and the Maya homeland there and gives a brief description of why the Maya left. We knew that we could not make a documentary about the violence in Guatemala, but we also felt that references to Guatemala were important, as were scenes from there. Next we brought in Jerónimo as someone who spoke English so that he could describe the community of Indiantown and the Maya there firsthand. With this scene completed, we had edited the first major section of the video, establishing for the viewer that the Maya were in the United States as refugees, showing the trauma of children who had witnessed violence in Guatemala, and providing the context of both Guatemala and Florida.

In the second part of the video we described life in Indiantown. This segment included interviews with Maya women about their work both in Indiantown and in Guatemala, an interview with the parish priest, Frank O'Loughlin, and the music of the Maya marimba band. While we were videotaping a woman at the laundromat, she began interviewing me. This happens frequently to anthropologists, but it is seldom shown as a part of doing anthropology. Alan Saperstein wanted to include the interview because it highlighted the constant dialogue between the people and us. I wanted to leave the scene out, as I felt that I stood out too much in the scene and took attention away from the purpose of the project. Alan prevailed, and the scene stayed in the documentary. In retrospect, this was a good decision. The scene provides a bit of humor and illustrates the active interest the Maya people of Indiantown take in others. It shows them not just as subjects of our videotaping but as active and curious people in their own right.

Following this scene we included a portion of a cooperative story told in Maya about the building of a road to San Miguel some fifty years ago. I thought it important to show Maya storytelling. The enthusiasm, interest, and commitment that the storytelling group shows contrasts with the somber and quiet talk that occurs when Spanish is spoken.

The next section of the videotape illustrates adaptation to Indiantown through children's activities, in and out of school, and a family meal in which we participated while we were videotaping in the community. The meal was itself cooperative: we cooked part of it along with the family in order to thank them for their help in the project. Our videographer, François Pietri, taped the rest of us eating with the family, and we decided to include ourselves in the section in order to show briefly some of our interaction with the people of the community. Taping the meal also allowed us to show changes in nutrition in the community and to discuss how families are isolated from each other in Indiantown, even though it is a relatively small community.

The documentary ends with footage of a soccer match between a team made up of Indiantown Maya and one made up of Mexican farmworkers. The soccer match again shows the Maya organizing themselves. It also helps to counter the impression of the Maya as being only farmworkers. We closed the program by returning to the marimba band as a symbol of Maya cultural identity in the community.

Maya in Exile is twenty-eight minutes long. Our goal was to give the video a quick pace and keep it under a half-hour long so that it could be viewed quickly and used in school and university classes. Certainly it could have been much longer. But we had decided to make several half-hour programs rather than one long program. We knew that we would have to return in subsequent years to document the changes in the community, so a brief video was more appropriate than a long one.

We were able to do the graphics, titles, and name keys for the video at a public television station, again working late at night when the equipment was not being used in regular production. We kept the graphics and effects of the program to a minimum to avoid distraction from the immediacy of the images.

Although the project team for *Maya in Exile* had a crew who worked exceptionally well together, regular conflicts, problems, and unresolved issues were still a part of the making of the video. First among these was the problem of funds. Although we begged, borrowed, and traded to get access to different broadcast quality equipment, the lack of a funded budget brought out conflicts among the crew. Some members, such as Denise Matthews, felt that they could only donate so much to the project and drifted away from the editing and final tape production. When the project was completed, we estimated that we had invested over three hundred hours in the production of the documentary. Because we all had other jobs and projects to work on, this meant that much of the work was done late at night. The program was edited between 11:00 P.M. and 4:00

A.M., for example, because that was the only time we could get together to edit.

The pressure of working nights in addition to our other employment exacerbated interpersonal conflicts during the editing process as well. It was here that aesthetic and professional opinions were most fragile. The creative control over final editing decisions, while still discussed by as many of the team members as were able to attend each night's session, had to rest finally with the director, Alan Saperstein. Because of the exchange of roles that characterized our filming and fund-raising, final aesthetic control was ceded to Saperstein, but only after several arguments and in spite of lingering resentments.

A second obstacle we faced was the distance between our field site, Indiantown in South Florida, and the site of our editing and final production, Gainesville and the University of Florida. Two hundred and fifty miles separate the two—by car, about five hours. This made it very difficult to return for further filming of the community context. For this, we had to rely on still photographs taken by one of our crew. Likewise, we had decided early on to make a documentary about the Maya people's lives here in the United States, and not about Guatemala. But because so many people in the documentary talked about their homeland, we needed to include imagery from Guatemala. We solved this problem by using still photographs that Jerónimo had taken of the Maya area before coming to the United States. This meant that the documentary lacked total live action, but we found that careful editing of still images enhanced the idea that Guatemala was now just a memory for the Maya of Indiantown.

A third issue was distribution. We had arranged to finish the project in time for a trip the marimba band took to Washington, D.C., in July 1985. They had been asked to take part in the Smithsonian Institution's annual United States Folk Festival as an example of an endangered tradition. Unfortunately, the museum staff was not willing to allow the sale of the tapes under the conditions of the festival.

Rather than go through a commercial distribution network, we decided to distribute the video ourselves as a way to bring the highest return to the community. Commercial distribution networks seldom realize a return for the principals on documentaries. We priced the half-hour version of the video at forty-five dollars and designed an advertising flyer to be sent around the country, to church groups, to all anthropology departments, and to friends. In addition, we distributed it wherever we could. We also explored the viability of joining a cooperative distribution company, but decided against this because the cooperative relied on individual film and video makers to do their own duplication, mailing, and distribution.

We were more successful in broadcasting the video on public television. Drawing on our contacts, we sent a broadcast tape version to several stations in Florida and across the United States. It was shown many times, and each time we asked stations for a reasonable broadcast fee, which was donated to the community.

A third distribution strategy we attempted was to use the state educational media office. State departments of education regularly buy the rights for educational videos. We were willing to sell the educational distribution rights to the state of Florida both because of the money the sale would bring in and because it would further publicize the lives of the Maya people in Florida. The official in charge of purchasing videos was at first enthusiastic about the documentary, but later said that it was too political to be purchased by the state.

The documentary was completed during the summer of 1985. It was shown first in the community to the Maya people and their comments were solicited. The showing of the documentary was an exciting event. Several hundred people came to the church hall in the town when the word went out that the documentary would be shown. We had translated the Kanjobal and Spanish to English in the course of producing the final version, so we asked a Kanjobal leader to translate the documentary back to Kanjobal for the assembled audience.

Several issues were brought up at the showing of the tape. Some members of the community did not like the references to the guerilla movement in the documentary. While many of the families in the community had suffered at the hands of the military in Guatemala, guerilla groups were also responsible for violence in the area. We attempted to keep the focus of the documentary on Maya adaptation to the United States, but this complex issue still surfaced through comments on it.

Second, the language of the video is English, with some Spanish and Kanjobal. The Kanjobal audience found the Kanjobal re-translation important; unfortunately we did not tape record the event, which might have led to a Kanjobal soundtrack. We learned from this experience, however: the last two videos, *La Mujer Maya* and *Salud Entre Dos Culturas*, were produced with both Maya and Spanish soundtracks.

The documentary has also been shown in Spain and Mexico. In these cases we also realized the need for a Spanish bilingual version. While it might seem to be easy to add such bilingual tracks to a documentary, however, in reality the amount of careful sound editing that went into the original makes such an effort almost as difficult as re-editing the entire documentary.

Although it would have been ideal to have been able to live in the community for a long period of time with the video crew, this is hardly possible in modern film and video work. Instead we relied on Jerónimo's presence in the community to establish our rapport as well as that of several graduate students in anthropology at the University of Florida who continue to work on other applied projects in the community.

Our vision of the Maya and the community of Indiantown was more complex when we came to make the second video, *Maya Fiesta*. The topic of the patronal fiesta of San Miguel for the video was suggested by a local Maya leader in Indiantown, Pascual Thomas, who suggested that we film something with traditional activities because he saw the children of the community losing a sense of who they were and what it meant to be Maya. *Maya Fiesta* is more sophisticated than *Maya in Exile* in portraying the complexity and conflicts within the community and representing the factionalism that is an important part of Maya life. We made an effort to include differences between Catholics, Seventh-Day Adventists, and traditionalists, as well as interethnic relations between the Maya, Mexicans, Haitians, and other people. But we were also careful to follow some of the same people we filmed for the first documentary, in some cases even when they had moved out of the community in search of work and the chance to raise their children away from the crowded housing and poor conditions of Indiantown.

I describe the making of *Maya in Exile* as a case example of using documentary techniques within an applied anthropology context. Applied anthropologists, more so than traditional anthropologists, are attuned to the importance of working in a team or small-group context. This project demonstrates not only the importance of consciously employing small-group dynamics to the organization of a project but also the need to use the knowledge and wisdom of the people one is working with to insure a successful project. The task groups that Maya people have developed for such diverse activities as *milpa* farming, storytelling, and marimba playing can be successfully adapted to the new task of making a video documentary.

Finally, the experience of making *Maya in Exile* and other programs illustrates the role that documentaries can play in applied, advocacy projects. The compelling imagery of a documentary can add to the written word and be useful in communicating with the public as well as officials. A colleague from Mexico, for example, took a copy of *Maya in Exile* to show to the United Nations High Commission on Refugee Affairs there. When the video was shown in Mexican Maya refugee communities, one refugee was pleased to see several of his friends— whom he thought had died in Guatemala—alive and well in Florida, and he began writing to them again. When the community group CORN-Maya applied for financial assistance in 1988, *Maya in Exile* was sent along with the grant applications. An agency official said that the reason the project was funded was because of the video, which gave a better picture of the community than a written description could.

One of the changes in both anthropology and documentary production of the 1990s is the shift from the authoritative voice of the outside observer to the knowledgeable voice of the insider. The long-term experience of working with the Maya of Indiantown on these video programs and other projects suggests that a better orientation includes collaborative work, whether in ethnography or in film and video production.

EIGHT

ALWAYS MAYA

The Maya are known as the largest indigenous society in North America, but as the decade of the 1990s emerged, they also became one of the most dispersed. Maya in Indiantown, Florida, are one part of a Maya diaspora that stretches from Central America through Canada.

The Maya are a people who interest travelers, tourists, historians, and anthropologists. Anthropologists have been fascinated with their prehistory. The rise of the Maya civilization, the nature of their architectural genius, and the complexities of their strategies of adaptation to the jungles and mountains of Mexico and Central America have spawned interest and research for more than a century (Coe 1986). Their complex social structure, ecological adaptations, and rich expressive life have served as an important case in the development of the world's civilizations. The record of the encounter, including books of prophecy such as the *Chilam Balam* (Edmonson 1986), codices of the years before conquest, and the book of counsel, or *Popol Vuh* (Tedlock 1985), constitute a literature that is unique in the world. The "ethnographic Maya," those Guatemalan villages studied by the early cultural anthropologists such as La Farge (La Farge and Byers 1931) and others, as well as the Chiapas Maya studied by the Harvard project in the 1960s (Vogt 1969;

Gossen 1974; Cancian 1965), have provided cultural anthropology with a rich record of local politics and culture. The Maya languages of Guatemala, including Jacaltec (Craig 1977) and Kanjobal (Martin 1977), have been a focus of study as well as a basis for community development in the 1970s (Arias 1990). The insurgency in Guatemala since 1954 and the effects of civil violence on indigenous communities have also become an important theme in the social sciences (Smith 1990). Maya refugees in Mexico (Stepputat 1989) and the adaptation of immigrants and refugees in the United States have received relatively little attention, but as communities like Indiantown become permanent locations for Maya immigrants, interest in Maya Americans is increasing (Chavez 1992).

The Maya have also been the source of splendid art through textiles. Maya weavings have graced the pages of fashion magazines, boutiques, and the bodies of tourists, travelers, and the general public for decades. If there is one adjective that has been applied to the Maya by tourists over the decades, it is "colorful." The Guatemalan Maya women's genius for color and weaving led to the development of textile cooperatives alongside the agricultural cooperatives in highland Maya villages in the 1970s.

When the increasing violence of the 1970s and 1980s struck the heart of the Guatemalan highlands, the Maya who had created this rich legacy were thrust into a different role. They ceased to be local villagers of ethnographic interest or skillful weavers of splendid textiles. They became victims, as indicated in the title of Beatriz Manz's book, *Refugees of a Hidden War* (1988), or casualties of repression, as in Carmack's *Harvest of Violence* (1988). They became immigrants exploited only for their labor in the Hollywood movie *El Norte* and in popular books on immigrants (Santoli 1988). And in places like the textile factories of Los Angeles, the orchards of Arizona, and the farms of Florida they became part of "the problem" of illegal aliens and immigration policy in the United States (Portes and Rumbant 1990).

The Maya of Indiantown have appeared on public radio and commercial television news reports, as well as in special stories in the national Sunday supplement magazine *Parade* (vol. 20, 1988). The stories about the Maya of Indiantown in local and regional newspapers in Florida as well as in the *New York Times* and other national papers have given the Maya of Indiantown a notoriety that is threatening to many people there. Some refugees fear that any publicity will lead to discovery and deportation, even though the Immigration and Naturalization Service has not targeted the community for raids against illegal immigrants. Still, the difficulties of leaving Guatemala and traveling across Mexico and the United States to Florida present such frightening risks that fear of deportation is real. That fear is an understandable adaptation to institutional danger, first realized through Guatemalan military institutional violence in the 1980s and since then through institutional dangers both in Guatemala and in the United States.

The adaptations that the Maya made to the United States over the first decade of their arrival were profound. They became adept at being migrant workers. They became targets of interpersonal violence through robberies, muggings, and fights. They also became distrusted and at times scorned by the resident U.S. community because of drunkenness, family violence, and the strain that thousands of immigrants put on the town. These kinds of changes can be seen at an institutional level through the fiesta of San Miguel, a key event of cultural intensification for the Maya of the United States. They can also be seen in the way that Maya people articulated with the bureaucracies of health care and social agencies.

As the Maya and other Guatemalans continue to immigrate

from Guatemala to the United States, a strategic adjustment is occurring in their expectations about life in the United States. One place where those changes can be seen in bold relief is in the organization and expression of the yearly festival of San Miguel. As discussed earlier, the fiesta is an important event in the yearly round of Indiantown and Immokalee in Florida, Los Angeles, and other centers of the Maya diaspora.

The first several years that the festival was held in the United States, it was both an occasion of cultural persistence and a way for the community to tell outsiders of their desire for peace and dignity in the United States. The speeches of the queens expressed these notions poignantly in three languages: Kanjobal, Spanish, and English. But gradually changes crept in.

Changes in the ideological orientation of the fiesta, which began with stress on Maya tradition and proceeded to include allusions to the insurgency of the 1980s, can be traced through the appearance of the T-shirts sold by the fiesta committee each year. The committee's first effort was a simple T-shirt that proclaimed the fiesta of San Miguel on one side and showed a stylized drawing of a marimba on the other. In the late 1980s, the quetzal began appearing on the fiesta T-shirts, and one year the shirts included the phrase from the *Popol Vuh*, "Let none be left behind the rest," reminiscent of the same phrase as it was used in the Guatemalan insurgent *Congreso de Unidad Campesino* manifesto of 1979, known as the *Declaración de Iximche:* "That all arise, that all be called. That there be neither one nor two groups among us who remain behind the rest!" (Arias 1990:254). By the 1990s, the ideology of the fiesta as expressed through the T-shirt slogans became one of ethnic pluralism. One of the T-shirt designs had flags of Guatemala, Mexico, Haiti, and the United States and bore the saying in Spanish: "Many different cultures in just one community, Indiantown, Florida." Another showed a map of Guatemala and

Mexico with a quetzal bird on it and proclaimed "Independence—Guatemex 1990."

As the numbers of Maya and other Guatemalan immigrants to the United States increased, the festival shifted in its emphasis. After several years of being held on the grounds of the Catholic church in Indiantown, after 1990 the festival was moved to a county park. This was in part due to the fact that the church began charging for the use of the grounds, electricity, and cafeteria. In addition, excessive beer drinking among festival participants cast a shadow on the use of the church grounds, and church officials preferred that the dances, raffles, and "cultural events" take place away from church property. The mass with baptisms was still held in the church and continued to constitute an important part of the fiesta. But everything else was held a mile a way in the county park.

The music of the fiesta has changed as well. Where the marimba had been the focal point of all activities earlier, a Mexican popular music band became the main source of entertainment. When people complained about the lack of marimba music, the marimba was brought out once or twice, but only as an addition to the Mexican band. The lack of this key cultural symbol was overshadowed by the great success of the reconstituted fiesta, as several thousand people attended over the two-day period.

By the early 1990s the festival of San Miguel was complemented by several other fiestas throughout the year for other villages and towns to which Guatemalan Maya had fled. Likewise, Indiantown became only one of the many places where the fiesta was celebrated. The Indiantown fiesta evolved from a primarily cultural event into an economic one as well. The fiesta began to be held in other agricultural communities beyond Indiantown. In Immokalee, a major community on the west coast of Florida, a smaller fiesta was held on a Friday night.

When I asked people who had been to that fiesta and the Indiantown fiesta about the differences, they said that the biggest one was in the sharing. In the fiesta in Immokalee, each of the principal families who planned the fiesta made a hundred *tamales* to give out. There were *tamales* everywhere, several people said. It was pointed out to me that in Indiantown, the *tamales* were good, but they were made and sold by a Mexican family; there were no Maya *tamales* to be had.

The fiesta has expressed the Maya immigrant community's changes and adaptations during the first ten years of life in the United States. It has remained a celebration that is uniquely Maya, but has changed from an attempt at reproducing the fiesta in Guatemala to a new fiesta that has a distinctive U.S. character. The fiesta has the advantage of being an institution where Maya control, while not complete, is at least a predominant part of the event. But the fiesta is only a once-a-year phenomenon. During the rest of the year the Maya have to adapt to other institutions, many of which are completely outside their control. While institutions such as health care are generally thought of as benign, they can also subvert Maya life in the United States.

As the community of Maya people becomes more differentiated in Indiantown, new problems have arisen. In the early 1980s, the Maya in Indiantown were largely the Kanjobal Maya of San Miguel Acatán, but by the end of the decade, people from other Maya groups had begun to arrive. The San Miguel Kanjobal people remained the majority, but they were joined by increasing numbers of people from Todos Santos, El Quiche, and other areas of the Maya highlands of Guatemala. A "pan-Maya" identity began to be forged by many community leaders. In 1991, representatives from the Guatemalan Maya community joined a communitywide celebration for the first time and were promoted by the local library association as a resource for the non-Maya part of the community instead of an embarrassment to it.

The community was dispersing as well. As more of the Maya received temporary or permanent immigration papers through the Immigration and Naturalization Service, and as they became more familiar with opportunities outside of Indiantown, they began moving to areas where housing was more plentiful and work was available. Young people who had been brought to the United States when they were children of eight and ten years old became adapted to migrant work by the time they were twenty.

As these changes came about, the Maya encountered problems that can be seen as institutional culture shock. One young Maya woman, Eulalia Fernandez, went to a clinic in a mid-Florida city because she was unhappy about her newborn baby. She was extremely dispirited, and her postpartum depression was compounded by a fear she had that African Americans were regularly pursuing her. The clinic sent her to a nearby hospital. At the hospital she could not make herself understood, so she was admitted to the psychiatric ward under the provisions of the Baker Act, which allows hospital personnel to put people in psychiatric wards if they are deemed dangerous to themselves or their children. It took most of a day for her husband, who was left with the couple's one-week-old baby, to locate her. At first the clinic would say only that she had been "released," and finally it took the services of a social worker from Indiantown to convince the clinic to explain what had happened to her. When the social worker called the hospital, the hospital staff said that the woman was "speaking in tongues" and was making no sense. It took over a week to get her released. In the meantime, her husband had to continue to work, find help to care for their children, and live with the realization that an institution like a hospital would quite literally lock up people who came there seeking help. When she was released, Eulalia Fernandez was told to go back to Guatemala where her fears of persecution by African Americans would be lessened. Ironically, she was sent to Guatemala where real persecutions continue.

Suspicion of institutions, of people, and of the culture of the United States has increased in the Maya community. By the 1990s the traditional Maya attitude of quiet resignation toward outsiders had been more and more replaced by an attitude of suspicion and wariness. The new home that the Maya had found was indeed a dangerous place. It was not only full of individual violence; even helping institutions like hospitals could not be trusted.

The fear and distrust of health care institutions developed out of many incidents like the one described above. On a daily basis, women who went to hospitals for illness, childbirth, or information often experienced attitudes of condescension and at times outright hostility. Stories of these experiences quickly spread throughout the community. Sometimes the cases stretched the credulity of outsiders who heard them. A case in point is that of a fifteen-year-old unwed mother, Magdalen Aguirre.

Magdalena had come to the United States only a year prior to becoming pregnant. When she gave birth to her daughter (in a different agricultural community than Indiantown), she was told by the hospital staff that a few tests had to be done on the child and that she was free to go home. The next day she returned to the hospital to learn that the child had been placed in a foster home. She was summoned to court for a hearing about her baby and was told in Spanish that the hospital did not think that she was "bonding" with the child. Since her primary language was Kanjobal, the responses she gave at the hearing were in limited Spanish.

Magdalena was in the United States without legal immigration papers, so the event of the hearing itself was traumatic. When the hearing officer asked what she planned to do, she said simply that she was going to return to Guatemala. When asked if she wanted her baby, she quietly said, "No." As an unwed mother, she was terrified of returning to Guatemala with a small child. She left the community and went into the migrant stream, working as an illegal alien for six months. When she returned the next fall, she contacted children's rights advocates to help her get her baby back. The advocacy group, Guardian Ad Litem, called and asked me to prepare an essay about Magdalena's case to help her get her baby back.

I pointed out in the report that as a member of an indigenous Maya community, Magdalena's history and tradition are significantly different from that of other local ethnic groups. She is not a "Hispanic migrant worker," but rather a Native American whose culture differs from that of the Hispanic societies of Mexico and Central America as much as it does from the societal norms of the United States. In addition, the terrorism and civil war in Guatemala necessarily condition her attitudes toward authority.

Guatemalan Maya girls are taught from a very early age to be productive and responsible members of society. Socialization for responsibility and commitment to ensuring the well-being of the community begins soon after birth, when godparents are expected to give a young girl small models of adult tools— books, weaving implements, needles and thread, and other utensils—as a part of the ceremony of Maya baptism. In the lowlands, this ceremony takes place when a child is placed astride the mother's hip. Along with the implements of the adult roles, the child's sponsors are expected to express their expectation that the child be responsible to her or his family and to the community.

Soon after a little girl begins to speak, she is expected to help with minor chores of the household economy, including the weaving. She will also be expected to help out with child care; infants are often left under the care of a four- or five-year-old girl for several hours at a time while her mother and sisters go about their household routines, only occasionally glancing in the direction of the child.

The most critical issue in socialization of Maya children has to do with their behavior toward authority figures, be they parents or other members of the community. The expected behavior is serious, polite silence. Children are expected to have fun and enjoy themselves, but in the presence of adults, they are expected to be courteous to the point of reticence, deferent to the point of complete silence, and humble. Proper interaction includes avoiding the direct gaze of adults, agreeing with what at times seem unreasonable statements, and moving out of the arena of adult action as quickly as possible. Anthropologist June Nash, an expert on highland Maya society, puts it this way:

> Socialization in the family provides the individual with the idiom for behaving in the wider community. The basic principles ordering behavior are respect and obedience toward those who are older, and care for those who are younger. Obedience, expressed by the verb *chhun* which means both to believe and to obey, is instilled by cultivating a sense of fear and shame. Fear is communicated by the threat or use of punishment. . . . Shame is aroused by ridicule, jeering, and chastising. A good child is a quiet child; questioning is discouraged either by refusing to answer the child or telling him to keep quiet. (Nash 1970:109)

When the child reaches teenage years, this quiet obedience becomes a strategy by which different work routines are learned. A teenage girl may learn to weave on factory looms, for example, by quietly watching an expert weaver for five or six months before undertaking the task herself. She then does so without the expected praise and emotional release that is often found in the United States when teenagers learn a new task. Manning Nash, in his book *Machine Age Maya* (1967), documents the efficacy of this kind of learning strategy and how it complements the overall pattern of socialization in Maya villages.

The bond between parents and children is much more extensive in Maya society than in the United States. It is expected that Maya children will remain in the household even after marriage, and grandparents take a major role in a young mother's life. It is common to find forty- and fifty-year-old daughters and sons living in the same household as their parents. Even parents-in-law are seen as "other parents" and are called "mother and father." The parents of both spouses attend baptisms and other events. The support of the family extends to cases when trouble arises—for example, if the girl is abandoned by her husband. Again, as June Nash puts it: "Even after marriage, the parents are concerned with maintaining their child's marital situation. . . . Parents usually accompany their children if they are called into court, and failure to attend is tantamount to admitting the guilt of the child" (Nash 1970:113).

In sum, Maya adolescence is an experience that is not really comparable with what most people in the United States think of when they think of that time of life. The concept of "childhood" as extending into the "teenage" years is not present in Maya society, where the expectations of being a productive member of a family and community are incrementally added to a young child's responsibilities until adulthood is reached. But those responsibilities do not result in the kind of independence that people in the United States expect of their young people. Instead, assuming adult roles includes strengthening the close bond with parents and other family members, and working in close harmony with the moral order, the rules of etiquette, and expectations of competence in the community.

Given this background, we can understand the psychological and cultural trauma experienced by many young immigrant women in the United States. The case of Magdalena, for example, can be understood in terms of these dimensions of family expectations and role behaviors. A young woman like Magdalena is first of all in a position of extreme shame, ridicule, and embarrassment for having a child outside of a traditional marriage. Maya girls are taught very little about sex and procreation, so a pregnancy from consensual intercourse or rape in the life of a teenage migrant worker is not surprising. The experience of not having a mother, sisters, and grandmothers around at birth is likewise traumatic. Traditional pregnancy knowledge is normally the realm of a lay midwife who, in addition to giving massages and reassurances, talks to pregnant women about what will happen during birth and postpartum behavior. Consequently, it is easy to see how such a fifteen-year-old girl, having given birth in the highly sophisticated, modern setting of a U.S. hospital, could consent to leave her baby with medical personnel. The values of obedience and silence and the hope of leaving the confusing world of U.S. health experts would lead a girl like Magdalena to leave without her child.

At the same time, the attachment that a woman develops with a child (often referred to as "bonding") can take time; it is not uncommon in the United States for a woman to be with a child weeks or even months before bonding occurs. Postpartum depression, the need for reinforcement and role models, and the emotional condition of a woman all contribute to the length of time it takes to form an attachment. In Central America, hospitals often require that parents and family members stay with a pregnant woman throughout labor and delivery, in part to lessen the need for nursing staff and in part to provide family support systems at this critical time. The attachment of mother and baby is, in the Central American context, a private process that involves the woman and her family. The sterile atmosphere of a U.S. hospital, on the other hand, can impede the process of attachment just as it is known to impede the onset of labor and delivery.

The psychological shock of the violence in Guatemala during the 1980s, of immigrating to the United States, and of losing contact with one's parents and community must also be considered if we are to understand this case. Refugees and survivors of disasters are often burdened by extreme guilt at having endured a tragedy in which others have perished. Such psychological trauma often results in an inability to make important decisions quickly, a "flat" emotional affect, and, among pregnant women, dystocia or the delay of labor at the term of a pregnancy. These aspects of Magdalena's case, compounded by the traditional value of quietness in the face of authority, could easily lead U.S. health and social service officials to misdiagnose the extent of her love for her child.

Still, when given the chance, Magdalena did not appear to want her child. One important reason for this impression was that Magdalena's first language is Kanjobal Maya. Questions and choices that had to be translated from English into a dialect of Spanish, which she understands poorly anyway, were, no doubt, very difficult to understand.

Beyond the important issue of language is her own perception of her self-worth and identity. The shock of leaving her own country and becoming a migrant worker in the United States led Magdalena to hide her vulnerability in a shell of solitude. Silence is also a sign of great respect to her, even when asked a direct question by an authority figure. As mentioned above, a young person would be harshly judged as incompetent in productive pursuits, immoral in family obligations, and a failure in

terms of community etiquette should she contemplate returning to her homeland and family with a child born out of wed-
lock. In addition, her quietness and passivity may also have
stemmed from the shame she may have felt at finding herself in
court without the support of her parents. In traditional Maya
communities, the failure of parents to appear in a court proceed-
ing is an admission by them of the "guilt" of the child. It is
doubtful that Magdalena could have shown assertive behavior
in such a situation by herself. Assertion and defense of one's
rights in Maya society is a cooperative, family endeavor, not
something that individuals undertake on their own.

Even the act of appearing before a figure of authority such as a
judge must be understood within her cultural context. Under
the Napoleonic system employed in Latin America, judges are
similar to prosecutors; the idea of a judge who listens to "both
sides" is outside that judicial tradition. Also, the use of tri-
bunals and courts in Guatemala as mechanisms for crushing
the insurgency has given them a terrible reputation. So when
Magdalena enters a courtroom for a hearing, her expectations
are much different from those of a U.S. citizen.

Contrasting with the severe and sometimes apparently un-
emotional behavior of Maya adolescents is the deep love that
they have for their children and their families. That love is not
expressed in ways that people in the United States expect:
kissing, for example, is a sign of ritual greeting, not a sign of
affection. Instead, affection is shown in the extensive time that
young Maya mothers spend with their children, talking with
them, talking about them, and encouraging their physical and
social development. It is also shown in the web of concern that
other family members or (in situations such as those in the
United States) housemates have for young children. That the
love of someone like Magdalena for her child is less effusive
than might be expected does not lessen its profundity.

Certainly, Magdalena has faced a difficult time for a fifteen-year-old mother. She lived through the experiences of fleeing the turmoil in Guatemala, becoming an undocumented alien in a strange and unintelligible country, and then having to leave her newborn at a hospital, all within one year. But she, like the larger Guatemalan Maya community in Florida, has made adjustments to life in the United States. Guatemalan families have taken on the responsibilities of teaching and sheltering younger women who have given birth. An informal but effective social network, involving those Guatemalan Maya who have been in the United States for several years, social agency workers, and church organizations, has developed. Through this network relatives or even people from the same mountain villages in Guatemala serve as surrogate parents in the United States to help young mothers cope with the demands of child socialization.

All these facts were presented during the new hearing on the case, which also included the use of a Kanjobal interpreter and an advocate from Guardian Ad Litem, the child advocacy association in Florida. As a result, Magdalena eventually was able to gain custody of her child, but by that time word of her experience and the capriciousness of the hospital staff had circulated throughout the Guatemalan Maya community. It served as a bitter lesson on institutional violence against Maya people in the United States.

It is no surprise that the immigration of the Kanjobal and other Maya to the United States, and especially to Florida, has brought about profound changes in the Maya society. The Maya have adapted to life in the United States in specific ways, including the forms of association they have created, the economic survival strategies of the community, and the communication networks established between the Maya of Indiantown and others in Guatemala, Mexico, and other parts of North America. This "strategic adaptation" (Safa and DuToit 1975) to an international cultural world has not always been successful. The complex cultural processes through which the Maya have lived since immigrating to the United States in the early 1980s are as challenging to the Maya people as they are to the community that has received them.

The dispersion of the Maya to the United States is unique in several respects as compared with other refugee movements. The Maya of the United States are not clear-cut, "recognized" refugees. Their status is still defined as either "legal" or "illegal." They lack refugee assistance in the form of social assistance programs, educational programs, and legal advocacy. Because refugee policy does not include the Maya, this channel for adapting to the institutions of the United States is closed. As a result many of the Maya live in a shadow world, taking care not to set themselves apart from other poor migrant workers lest they become targets for deportation. Workers who are not paid for labor do not report such abuses for fear of being turned in to immigration authorities. Families who are eligible for medical or nutritional assistance do not make use of it for fear that their children, born in the United States, will be taken away from them. One family was incorrectly told by a neighbor that the U.S. government gets names of Guatemalans off social assistance lists and then takes their children away. The cases recounted earlier make such fears real, and so such rumors are heeded.

As of 1992, voluntary repatriation is not an effective strategy for the Maya. A report on repatriation efforts by the Guatemalan government through 1990 shows a dismal record of success (AVANCSO 1990). Indeed, one of the principal investigators for that study, anthropologist Myrna Mack, was killed in Guatemala City as the report was being released. Except for brief visits, then, to visit family or help others emigrate, the Maya cannot go back; but at the same time, as we just saw, they have not been able to integrate themselves into U.S. society. Consequently, the Maya are able to adapt strategically in ways that keep them at a level of survival but not at a level of either full integration or success.

A model of refugee adaptation well known in the literature on displaced people is that proposed by Scudder and Colson (1982). Their model is a linear one in which people flee from a natural or social disaster and finally reach a host country, where a period of community building and adjustment eventually leads to integration into the new society or country. The Maya of the United States show a different pattern. In their pattern of adaptation, a new social and cultural system is created out of the experience of leaving Guatemala under severe political and economic strife. Their new community in Indiantown is part of a new social formation that includes a great deal of mobility and communication between a series of small communities like Indiantown, both inside and outside the United States. It also includes a replenishment of cultural knowledge through the continuous arrival of new refugees and immigrants from Guatemala and the clandestine visits of U.S. Maya back to Guatemala. The model of strategic adaptation that the Indiantown Maya present is one of moving from a community that is localized within Guatemala to an international indigenous community. This international indigenous community is connected to the migrant labor streams of the United States and Canada and also incorporates refugee enclave communities in Mexico and Guatemala. This system of adaptation includes increasing connections to world ethnic political movements, tempered by the factionalism that has characterized Maya communities throughout their history.

This model of refugee adaptation differs from other descriptions of immigrant enclave communities proposed by Portes and Stepick (1985) in that the Maya have become an enclave within places like Indiantown and at the same time have strengthened ties to other communities. Theirs is not an adaptation to a single site so much as an adaptation to many sites across national boundaries in North America. This process leads to the creation of multicultural communities rather than the communities of assimilation or enclaves that are often proposed as the model of immigrant adaptation (Scudder and Colson 1982; Portes and Rumbant 1990).

The experiences of the Maya of Guatemala as they become a part of the broader society of the United States at the end of the twentieth century have taken place in the context of the largest movement of displaced people in recent history. An estimated 17 million people worldwide were refugees by the beginning of the 1990s. The story of the Maya in Florida and elsewhere in the United States has elements in common with other immigrant and refugee groups, but it also is unique. The Maya of the United States represent an indigenous migration, whereas other immigrants from Mexico and Central America have been drawn from mestizo populations. The Maya sought out ways of gaining acceptance for their plight and assistance for the problems they encountered as refugees. Along with networks of relatives and fictive kin, the Maya also used networks of religious workers and anthropologists.

The Maya who came to the United States had extensive experience with anthropologists; many had been subjects of studies, others had served as fieldwork assistants, and some, like Jerónimo Camposeco, had trained in anthropology at the university level. A few, such as Victor Montejo (1987, 1991), continued their studies in the United States. But for the majority of Maya refugees, such a strategy of education was not available. Instead, they quickly moved into economic niches such as agricultural work, construction work, and services within the informal economy. The connection to anthropology remained, however, as community leaders continued to seek support through the work of anthropologists.

The applied work that informed much of our research with the Maya of Florida was collaborative. The different directions the projects took were responses to the issues faced in the community and the availability of anthropologists to work in the community. The issue of political asylum, which informed early work with the community, gave way to issues in education, health care, and cultural persistence. Students with skills in areas outside Maya studies, such as medicine or infant development, were attracted to doing work in a "third world" community located in South Florida. Fieldwork in Indiantown was difficult: one fieldworker contracted tuberculosis in the unsanitary conditions of poverty there; another was harassed by the police; and others found the stress of the life-and-death problems of the Maya overwhelming. Still, applied anthropology flourished. Non-Maya residents of good will welcomed the work and opened their doors to those of us who came to live in the community for periods from several weeks to several years. Unlike other applied anthropology projects, the work with the Maya has been continuous and has adapted to the changes in circumstance caused by events in Guatemala, changes in immigration law, and occurrences in the local community.

Support for the Maya spread to church and civic organizations, county government offices, and institutions such as clinics and hospitals. While many residents still resented the influx of this large and confusing group of immigrants, others began to accept their presence and to work with them. Maya children, born in the United States, became fluent in English and became the second generation of Maya Americans.

BIBLIOGRAPHY

Adams, Richard N. 1953. "Notes on the Application of Anthropology." *Human Organization* 12(2): 10–14

———. 1979. *Crucifixion by Power.* Austin: University of Texas Press.

Aguirre Beltran, Gonzalo. 1967. *Regiones de Refugio: El Desarrollo de la Communidad y el Proceso de Dominical en Mestizo America.* Mexico: Instituto Nacional Indigenista.

Anderson, Benedict. 1983. *Imagined Communities: Reflections on the Origin and Spread of Nationalism.* London: Verso.

Annis, Sheldon. 1987. *God and Production in a Guatemalan Town.* Austin: University of Texas Press.

Arias, Arturo. 1990. "Changing Indian Identity: Guatemala's Violent Transition to Modernity." *Guatemalan Indians and the State: 1540–1988,* ed. Carol Smith. Austin: University of Texas Press.

Asch, Timothy. 1979. "Making a Film Record of the Yanomamo Indians of Southern Venezuela." *Perspectives on Film* 2:4–9.

Ashabranner, Brent, and Paul Conklin. 1986. *Children of the Maya.* New York: Dodd, Mead and Company.

Asociación para el Avance de las Ciencias Sociales (AVANCSO). 1990. Guatemala *Assistance and Control: Policies Toward Internally Displaced Populations in Guatemala.* Washington, D.C.: Center for Immigration Policy and Refugee Assistance, Georgetown University.

Barth, Frederik. 1969. *Ethnic Groups and Boundaries.* Boston: Little, Brown.

Bateson, Gregory, and Margaret Mead. 1941. *Balinese Character.* New York: Museum of Natural History.

Becker, Howard S. 1975. "Photography and Sociology." *Afterimage,* May/June: 22–32.

Bernard, H. Russell. 1988. *Methods in Anthropology.* Beverly Hills: Sage Publications.

Bizairo Uzpán, Ignacio. 1985. *Campesino: The Diary of a Guatemalan Indian*. Translated and edited by James Sexton. Tucson: University of Arizona Press.

Boothby, Neil. 1986. "Children and War." *Cultural Survival Quarterly* 10(4).

Brintnall, Douglas E. 1979. *Revolt Against the Dead: The Modernization of a Maya Community in the Highlands of Guatemala*. New York: Gordon and Breach.

Bunzel, Ruth. 1952. *Chichicastenango: A Guatemalan Village*. American Ethnological Society, Publication No. 22. Seattle: University of Washington Press.

Burns, Allan F. 1980. "Interactive Features in Yucatec Mayan Oral Narratives." *Language and Society* 9:309–17.

———. 1983. *An Epoch of Miracles: Oral Literature of the Yucatec Maya*. Austin: University of Texas Press.

———. 1988. "Kanjobal Maya Resettlement: Indiantown, Florida." *Cultural Survival Quarterly* 12(4): 41–45.

———. 1989a. "Internal and External Identity Among Kanjobal Refugees in Florida." *Conflict, Migration, and the Expression of Ethnicity*, ed. Nancie Gonzalez and C. McCommon, pp. 46–59. Boulder: Westview Press.

———. 1989b. "The Maya of Florida." *Refugee World* 9(4): 20–26.

———. 1990. "Immigration, Ethnicity, and Work in Indiantown, Florida." *Occasional Paper No. 8 of the University of Florida Center for Latin American Studies*. Gainesville, Fla.: Center for Latin American Studies.

———. 1992. "Modern Yucatec Maya Oral Literature." In *On the Translation of Native American Literatures*, ed. Brian Swann. Washington, D.C.: Smithsonian Institution Press.

———. Forthcoming. "Toward a Dialogic Anthropology: The Story of Lynch Hammock." In *Toward a Dialogic Anthropology*, ed. Dennis Tedlock and Bruce Manheim.

Burns, Allan F., and Jerónimo Camposeco. 1991. "El Pueblo de los Indios: Indiantown, Florida." Paper presented at the 1991 Latin American Studies Association Meeting, Washington, D.C.

Burns, Allan F., and Alan Saperstein. 1985. *Maya in Exile* (video program). Distributor: CORN-Maya, Indiantown, Fla.

———. 1988. *Maya Fiesta* (video program). Distributor: CORN-Maya, Indiantown, Fla.

Camara, Fernando B. 1952. "Religious and Political Organization." In *Heritage of Conquest*, ed. Sol Tax, pp. 142–73. Glencoe, Ill.: Free Press.

Cameon, Randi. 1991. *La Mujer Maya: Salud Prenatal* (video program). Distributor: Southeast Florida March of Dimes, West Palm Beach, Fla.

Camposeco, Jeronimo, Antonio Silvestre, and Ellen Davey. 1986. "Report of the Deportation Hearings Held in Miami Courts on June 23, 24, and 25, 1986." Manuscript, CORN-Maya archives, Indiantown, Fla.

Cancian, Frank. 1965. *Economics and Prestige in a Maya Community: The Religious Cargo System in Zinacantan.* Stanford: Stanford University Press.

Carmack, Robert M. 1981. *The Quiche Mayas of Utatlán: The Evolution of a Highland Guatemalan Kingdom.* Norman: University of Oklahoma Press.

———. 1983. "Spanish-Indian Relations in Highland Guatemala: 1800–1944." In *Spaniards and Indians in Southeastern Mesoamerica,* ed. Murdo MacLeod and Robert Wasserstrom, pp. 215–52. Lincoln: University of Nebraska Press.

———, ed. 1988. *Harvest of Violence: The Mayan Indians and the Guatemalan Crisis.* Norman: University of Oklahoma Press.

Chambers, Erve. 1987. "Applied Anthropology in the Post-Vietnam Era: Anticipations and Ironies." *Annual Reviews of Anthropology* 16:309–37.

Chavez, Leo. 1992. *Shadowed Lives: Undocumented Immigrants in American Society.* Fort Worth, Tex.: Harcourt Brace Jovanovich College Publishers.

Coe, Michael. 1986. *The Maya.* New York: Praeger.

Collier, Malcolm, and John Collier, Jr. 1986. *Visual Anthropology.* Albuquerque: University of New Mexico Press.

Connover, Ted. 1987. *Coyote: A Journey Through the Secret World of America's Illegal Aliens.* New York: Vintage Books.

Craig, Colette. 1977. *The Structure of Jacaltec.* Austin: University of Texas Press.

Davis, Shelton H. 1970. "Land of Our Ancestors: A Study of Land Tenure and Inheritance in the Highlands of Guatemala." Ph.D. dissertation, Harvard University.

Davis, Shelton, and Julie Hodson. 1982. *Witness to Political Violence in Guatemala: The Suppression of a Rural Development Movement.* Boston: Oxfam America, Impact Audit no. 2.

De la Fuente, Julio. 1967. "Ethnic Relationships." *Handbook of Middle American Anthropology: Social Anthropology* 6:432–48.

De Vos, George, and Lola Romanucci-Ross. 1982. *Ethnic Identity:*

Cultural Continuities and Change. Chicago: University of Chicago Press.

Dobyns, Henry F., P. L. Doughty, and H. D. Lasswell. 1971. *Peasants, Power and Applied Social Change.* Beverly Hills: Sage Publications.

Dorman, Sherri. 1986. "Applied Anthropology with Haitian Immigrants." Non-thesis report, Department of Anthropology. Gainesville: University of Florida.

Doughty, Paul L. 1987. "Against the Odds: Collaboration and Development at Vicos." In *Collaborative Research and Social Change,* ed. David D. Still and Joan Schensul. Boulder: Westview Press.

———. 1988. "Crossroads for Anthropology: Human Rights in Latin America." In *Human Rights and Anthropology,* ed. Theodore E. Downing and Gilbert Kushner, pp. 43–71. Cambridge, Mass.: Cultural Survival.

Early, John D. 1982. "A Demographic Survey of Contemporary Guatemalan Maya: Some Methodological Implications for Anthropological Research." In *Heritage of Conquest: Thirty Years Later,* ed. Carl Kendall, John Hawkins, and Laurel Bosser, pp. 73–89. Albuquerque: University of New Mexico Press.

Eddy, Elizabeth, and William Partridge, eds. 1986. *Applied Anthropology in the Americas* (second edition). New York: Columbia University Press.

Edmonson, Munro. 1986. *Heaven Born Merida and Its Destiny: The Chilam Balam of Chumayel.* Austin: University of Texas Press.

Elmendorf, Mary. 1976. *Nine Mayan Women.* New York: Schocken Books.

Falla, Ricardo S. J. 1983. "The Massacre at the Rural Estate of San Francisco—July, 1982," *Cultural Survival Quarterly,* 7(1): 43–44.

Ferris, Elizabeth G. 1987. *The Central American Refugees.* New York: Praeger Publishers.

Flocks, Joan. 1988. "Haitians and African Americans in a Small Florida Town." Master of arts thesis, Center for Latin American Studies. Gainesville, Fla.: University of Florida.

Foster, George M. 1969. *Applied Anthropology.* Boston: Little, Brown.

Frelick, William. 1991. *Running the Gauntlet: The Central American Journey Through Mexico.* Washington, D.C.: U.S. Committee for Refugees.

Fried, Jonathan, ed. 1983. *Guatemala in Rebellion: Unfinished Histories.* New York: Grove Press.

Garrett, Wilbur E. 1989. "La Ruta Maya." *National Geographic* 176(4): 424–79.

Gossen, Gary. 1974. *Chamulas in the World of the Sun: Time and Space in a Maya Community.* Chicago: University of Chicago Press.

Hawkins, John P. 1984. *Inverse Images: The Meaning of Culture, Ethnicity and Family in Post-Colonial Guatemalan Society.* Albuquerque: University of New Mexico Press.

Heider, Karl. 1976. *Ethnographic Film.* Austin: University of Texas Press.

Helton, Arthur. 1989. "Asylum and Refugee Protection in the Bush Years." *World Refugee Survey, 1988.* Washington, D.C.: World Refugee Committee.

Henry, Jules. 1963. *Culture Against Man.* New York: Vintage Books.

Holmberg, Alan, Henry F. Dobyns, et al. 1962. "Community and Regional Development: the Joint Cornell-Peru Experiment." *Human Organization* 21:107–24.

Holmberg, Alan, Mario Vasquez, et al. 1965. "The Vicos Case: Peasant Society in Transition," *American Behavioral Scientist* 8(7) :3–33.

Kaufman, Terrence. 1974. *Idiomas de Mesoamerica.* Guatemala: Editorial José de Pineda Ibarra.

La Farge, Oliver. 1940. "Maya Ethnology: The Sequence of Cultures." In C. L. Hay et al., eds., *The Maya and Their Neighbors,* pp. 281–91. New York: Appleton-Century Co.

———. 1947. *Santa Eulalia: The Religion of a Cuchumatán Indian Town.* Chicago: University of Chicago Press.

La Farge, Oliver, and Douglas Byers. 1931. *The Year Bearer's People.* Middle American Research Institute, Publication no. 3. New Orleans: Tulane University.

Lovell, W. George. 1985. *Conquest and Survival in Colonial Guatemala: A Historical Geography of the Cuchumatán Highlands. 1500–1821.* Kingston, Ontario: McGill-Queen's University Press.

———. 1988. "Surviving Conquest: The Maya of Guatemala in Historical Perspective." *Latin American Research Review* 23:25–57.

Lynch, B. D. 1981. *The Vicos Experiment: A Study of the Impacts of the Cornell-Peru Project in a Highland Community.* Washington, D.C.: Agency for International Development.

MacLeod, Murdo J. 1973. *Spanish Central America: A Socioeconomic History, 1520–1720.* Berkeley and Los Angeles: University of California Press.

Manz, Beatriz. 1988. *Refugees of a Hidden War: The Aftermath of Counterinsurgency in Guatemala.* Albany: State University of New York Press.

———. 1989. *Repatriation and Reintegration: An Arduous Process in Guatemala,* Washington, D.C.: Center for Immigration Policy and Refugee Assistance, Georgetown University.

Marcus, George E., and Michael Fischer. 1986. *Anthropology as Cultural Critique.* Chicago: University of Chicago Press. Martin County, Florida. 1985. "Comprehensive Plan." Manuscript.

———. 1987. "Regional Comprehensive Plan." Manuscript.

Martin, Laura E. 1977. "Positional Roots in Kanjobal (Maya)." Ph.D. dissertation, University of Florida Department of Anthropology, Gainesville, Fla.

Mead, Margaret. 1975. "Visual Anthropology in a Discipline of Words." In *Principles of Visual Anthropology,* ed. George Hockings. The Hague: Mouton.

Menchu, Rigoberta. 1984. *I, Rigoberta Menchu: An Indian Woman in Guatemala.* Edited and introduced by Elizabeth Burgos-Debray; translated by Ann Wright. London: Verso.

Michaels, Eric, and Francis Jupurrula Kelly. 1984. "The Social Organization of an Aboriginal Video Workplace." *Australian Aboriginal Studies* 1:26–34.

Miralles, Maria. 1986. "Health Seeking Behaviors of Guatemalan Refugees in South Florida." Master's thesis, University of Florida Department of Anthropology, Gainesville, Fla.

———. 1989. *A Matter of Life and Death: Health Seeking Behaviors in a Maya Immigrant Community.* New York: AMS Press.

Montejo, Victor, 1987. *Testimony: Death of a Guatemalan Village.* Willimantic, Conn.: Curbstone Press.

———. 1991. *The Bird Who Cleans the World and Other Mayan Fables.* Willimantic, Conn.: Curbstone Press.

Nash, June. 1970. *In the Eyes of Their Ancestors: Belief and Behavior in a Maya Community.* Cambridge: Harvard University Press.

Nash, Manning. 1967. *Machine Age Maya: Industrialization of a Guatemalan Community.* Chicago: University of Chicago Press.

———. 1989. *The Cauldron of Ethnicity in the Modern World.* Chicago: University of Chicago Press.

North, David, and Anna M. Portz. 1988. "Through the Maze: An Interim Report on the Alien Legalization Program." Manuscript. Washington, D.C.: TransCentury Development Associates.

Nuñez del Prado, Oscar. 1973. *Kayo Chico: Applied Anthropology in an Indian Community.* Chicago: University of Chicago Press.

Padgett, T. 1989. "Walking on Ancestral Gods." *Newsweek,* October 9.

Painter, James. 1987. *Guatemala: False Hope, False Freedom.* London: Latin American Bureau.

Paul, Lois, and Benjamin D. Paul. 1975. "The Maya Midwife as Sacred Professional: A Guatemalan Case." *American Ethnologist* (2):707–26.

Pelto, Pertti J., and Gretel H. Pelto. 1976. *Anthropological Research: The Structure of Inquiry.* New York: Harper and Row.

Peñalosa, Fernando. 1988. "Incipient Trilingualism Among Mayans in Los Angeles." Paper presented at the 14th International Congress of the Latin American Studies Association, New Orleans, La.

Portes, Alejandro, and Ruben Rumbant. 1990. *Immigrant America: A Portrait.* Berkeley: University of California Press.

Portes, Alejandro, and Alex Stepick. 1985. "Unwelcome Immigrants: The Labor Market Experience of 1980 (Mariel) Cuban and Haitian Refugees in South Florida." *American Sociological Review* 50:493–514.

Press, Irwin. 1969. "Ambiguity and Innovation: A Model for the Genesis of the Culture Broker." *American Anthropologist* 71:205–17.

Reina, Ruben. 1974. "The Structural Context of Religious Conversion in Petén, Guatemala: Status, Community and Multicommunity." *American Ethnologist* 1(1): 157–91.

Ressler, Edward, Neil Boothby, and D. Steibock. 1988. *Unaccompanied Children: Care and Protection in Wars, Natural Disasters, and Refugee Movements.* New York: Oxford University Press.

Rocha, Maria Cecilia. 1991a. "Health Practices Among Guatemalan Maya Women in Indiantown." Master of arts thesis, Center for Latin American Studies, University of Florida.

———. 1991b. *Salud Entre Dos Culturas* (video program). Distributor: Presbyterian Women's Thank Offering, Lexington, Ky.

Rollwagen, Jack. 1988. *Anthropological Filmmaking.* New York: Harwood Publishers.

Royce, Anya. 1982. *Ethnic Identity: Strategies of Diversity.* Bloomington: Indiana University Press.

Safa, Helen, and B. D. DuToit, eds. 1975. *Migration and Urbanization: Models and Adaptive Strategies.* Chicago: Aldine.

Santoli, Anthony. 1988. *New Americans: An Oral History.* New York: Viking Publishers.

Scudder, Thayer, and Elizabeth Colson. 1982. "From Welfare to Development: A Conceptual Framework for the Analysis of Dislocated Peoples." In *Involuntary Migration and Resettlement: The Problems and Responses of Dislocated People,* ed. Art Hansen and Anthony Oliver-Smith. Boulder, Colo.: Westview Press.

Simon, Jean-Marie. 1987. *Guatemala: Eternal Spring, Eternal Tyranny.* New York: Norton.

Smith, Carol. 1990. "Introduction: Social Relations in Guatemala over Time and Space." In *Guatemalan Indians and the State: 1540 to 1988*, ed. C. Smith, pp. 1–27. Austin: University of Texas Press.

Smith, Hubert. 1979. "A Personal Comment on the Quality of 'Human Documentaries,'" *Society for the Anthropology of Visual Communication Newsletter* 7(2): 3–4.

———. 1985. *The Living Maya* (video program). Distributor: University of California Extension Media Services, Los Angeles.

Spradley, James. 1979. *The Ethnographic Interview.* New York: Holt, Rinehart, and Winston.

———. 1980. *Participant Observation.* New York: Holt, Rinehart, and Winston.

Stearns, David. 1986. "Using Ethnography to Link School and Community in Rural Yucatan." *Anthropology and Education Quarterly* 17(1): 6–24.

Stepputat, Finn. 1989. "Self-Sufficiency and Exile in Mexico." Geneva, Switzerland: United Nations Research Institute for Social Development, Discussion Paper 9.

Tax, Sol. 1952. *Heritage of Conquest: The Ethnology of Middle America.* Glencoe, IL: Free Press.

Tedlock, Barbara. 1982. *Time and the Highland Maya.* Albuquerque: University of New Mexico Press.

Tedlock, Dennis. 1983. *The Spoken Word and the Work of Interpetation.* Philadelphia: University of Pennsylvania Press.

———. 1985. *The Popol Vuh.* New York: Simon and Schuster.

Todorov, Tzvetan. 1984. *The Conquest of America.* New York: Harper and Row.

United States President's Advisory Committee for Refugees. 1986. *World Refugee Survey 1986.* Washington D.C.: United States Committee for Refugees.

Valencia, Eliecer. 1984. *Guatemalan Refugees in Mexico, 1980–1984.* New York: Americas Watch Committee.

Vogt, Evan Z. 1969. *Zinacantan: A Maya Community in the Highlands of Chiapas.* Cambridge: Harvard University Press.

Wagley, Charles. 1949. *The Social and Religious Life of a Guatemalan Village.* Memoirs of the American Anthropological Association, no. 71. Menasha, Wis.: American Anthropological Association.

Warner, L. Lloyd. 1956. *Yankee City.* Chicago: University of Chicago Press.

Washington Office on Latin America. 1988. *Who Pays the Price? The Cost of War in the Guatemalan Highlands.* Washington, D.C.: Washington Office on Latin America.

Wolf, Eric R. 1957. "Closed Corporate Peasant Communities in Meso-america and Central Java." *Southwestern Journal of Anthropology* 13(1): 1–18.

———. 1982. *Europe and the People Without History.* Berkeley: University of California Press.

Worth, Sol, and John Adair. 1970. *Through Navajo Eyes.* Bloomington: Indiana University Press.

Zetter, Roger. 1988. "Refugees and Refugee Studies: A Label and an Agenda." *Refugee Studies* 1:1–6.

Ziller, Robert. 1990. *Photographing the Self.* Newbury Park, Calif.: Sage Publications.

Zolberg, Arishtide, Astri Suhrke, and Sergio Aguayo. 1989. *Escape from Violence: Conflict and the Refugee Crisis in the Developing World.* New York: Oxford University Press.

INDEX